NO EASY MONEY

MONEY

A GAMBLER'S DIARY

NO EASY MONEY
A GAMBLER'S DIARY

DAVE NEVISON
WITH DAVID ASHFORTH

RACING POST

Published in 2008 by Racing Post
Compton, Newbury, Berkshire RG20 6NL

A catalogue record for this book is available from the British Library.

ISBN 978-1-905156-48-1

Designed by Elaine Prestlien @ Prestlien Design

Printed in the UK by CPI William Clowes Beccles NR34 7TL

CONTENTS

CHAPTER ONE

TARGETING CHELTENHAM

This summer, I aim to make £80,000 – £80,000 from gambling on horses, from the opening day of the Cheltenham Festival in March to the closing day of Doncaster's St Leger Festival in September. Six months. I don't think it's an unreasonable target.

Actually, I don't want to make £80,000, I want to make half a million pounds. And that isn't an unrealistic ambition, either, because I'm going to have a serious crack at the Tote's Scoop6 and Jackpot. I want to win enough to make a life-changing difference and my best chance of doing that isn't by grinding away every day but by scooping a big pot. I think I can do it.

Jackpots aside, the way to make decent money betting on horses is to concentrate on the big meetings. For me, the biggest factor in determining whether I win or lose is the margin I'm betting against, and the margin is smallest at the big meetings. At the Cheltenham Festival, the Mecca of the jumps season, there is terrific competition between every major betting operator, and a lot of minor ones, too. The competition ensures that bookmakers bet to very narrow margins. If you know what you are doing, and you put in the necessary work, you can come out in front.

I do know what I'm doing, I intend to put in the work, and I will come out in front. I can and I will, as Dale Carnegie once said, before he died.

*

CHELTENHAM
MONDAY MARCH 10

My mate has got a very nice settee in his apartment in Cheltenham. For the next few nights, that settee will be my home. It isn't as nice as the beds in the Dormy House Hotel, near Broadway, where I usually stay for the Festival. On the other hand, the settee doesn't cost £250 a night, and it's nearer the Montpelier Wine Bar. So why have I booked into the Dormy House Hotel again?

Not that I'm planning to spend much time in the Montpelier. My plan is to steer clear of the high jinks and devote a clear head to the task in hand. The first task is to be at the racecourse on Monday evening for a *Racing Post* forum. It's a chance to wander around the racecourse, watch people make their final preparations for the start of the Festival, and enjoy anticipating tomorrow's atmosphere. It's quiet now but it will soon be bustling and noisy and excited.

The forum went well and then it was on to another, for Betfair radio. When you are on a panel with Mark Winstanley, journalist and tipster, you know it's going to be an easy ride, because Mark never stops talking, or swearing. The man in charge of the bleep machine is the busiest man there. Winstanley just can't stop himself. My language isn't too good and gets worse after a couple of beers but when I've got a microphone in front of me I do manage some self-censorship. Mark seems to find that impossible, which sometimes has hilarious consequences. He reminds me of the character Fred Scuttle in those old Benny Hill shows.

TUESDAY MARCH 11

By the time I get to the press room on the first day, there's not an awful lot to do. Most of my betting has already been done. Usually, my idea of an ante-post bet is to back a horse at 10am when it's running at 2.30pm but my betting partner, Mark Smith, is more into ante-post betting, especially for Cheltenham, where the markets are very mature by the day of the race.

The best ante-post bet, the one to cover the week's expenses, was the £1,400 we had at just worse than even money that the meeting would open with the going officially good to soft. My theory states that, if the ground is firm on the opening day of the Festival, it will officially be good to soft and, if the going is heavy, it will also officially be good to soft. The official description might be changed after the first race but, unless there is a deluge overnight, the going will definitely be good to soft because that's what everyone wants it to be. Tuesday has arrived and, sure enough, the going is officially good to soft. We're over a grand up and nothing's happened yet.

Mark is the king of our Cheltenham ante-post book. He's backed Noland for today's Arkle Chase, at 12-1. As Noland is now the 7-4 favourite, it means we can play on some of the others in the race. I've had £700 on Sizing Europe for the Champion Hurdle, at 14-1. He's now 2-1 favourite. I've also backed Harchibald at 8-1. Everyone knows that Harchibald cruises up on the bridle then doesn't find anything but the race isn't strong this year and at some point during it

Harchibald will trade at shorter than 2-1 in-running. Then I'll lay him. That's the theory, anyway.

Last year, on the spread betting markets, we sold SPs at 285 points for a lot of money. After four of the meeting's 24 races, the SPs already totalled 109.5 points and suicide beckoned. In the end, the total was a not too disastrous 306 points but it didn't do my nerves, or my equilibrium, much good. I've still got faith in the theory that led me to sell SPs last year, the theory being that, when a fourth day was added to the Festival, the effect was to reduce the competitiveness of some races, thereby increasing the likelihood of them being won by horses near the front of the market. We've sold SPs again, but not for as much as last year, when the bet was on my mind too much. I think it coloured my judgement from race to race, which wasn't helpful. I don't want that to happen again. We've also bought favourites and sold the Paul Nicholls index, betting that he won't have as successful a meeting as many people believe.

Nicholls is champion jumps trainer and, through his column in the *Racing Post* and television appearances, has a very high profile. As a result, a lot of his horses are likely to start at shorter prices than their chance of winning justifies.

I've got another theory. While Nicholls' horses will run their races in the championship events, I think they are less likely to shine in the Festival's handicap races because most of them haven't been targeted specifically at Cheltenham but have been running in the big handicap races on Saturdays throughout the season, often very successfully. It means that better handicapped horses will be running against them and the very high expectations for his horses in the championship races will have to be met to make up the quoted spread. Nicholls will probably have to have the first and second in both the Champion Chase and Gold Cup.

I've been on the panels of several Cheltenham preview events and, at all of them, I've said that, having watched Tidal Bay plough through the fences on his most recent run, at Doncaster, I felt sure that he'd end up on the floor in the Arkle Chase. For good measure, I said that Tidal Bay's trainer, Howard Johnson, wasn't a man whose public statements should be taken too seriously, because I think he likes to walk the press up the garden path.

This morning, I had yet another look at the race and reached the conclusion that there were only two horses in it. One was Noland and the other – well, that was Tidal Bay. If Noland was as good as Paul Nicholls, his trainer, said he was then he'd win and if Tidal Bay stood up he'd outclass every horse except Noland. Admittedly, I also thought there was a good chance that Tidal Bay would fall over but that was more than factored into his price. We could get 8-1, and we'd got a long price against Noland ante-post. So I ended up backing Tidal Bay. After an early mistake he didn't just jump safely, he put in an exhibition round while Noland clearly wanted further. Of course, I then blamed myself for not having had a bigger bet, in the way that you do.

I did think of increasing my bet on Harchibald in the next race, the Champion Hurdle, still with a view to laying him in-running. Luckily, I didn't, because he ran badly from start to finish. I never got an opportunity to lay him. I did have a bit on the winner, Katchit, partly because we were still in the Jackpot but didn't have Katchit in our perm.

Like a lot of people, I had fallen for the line that five-year-olds don't win the Champion Hurdle, especially if, like Katchit, they won the Triumph Hurdle the previous season. The last Triumph Hurdle winner to win the following year's Champion Hurdle was Persian War in 1968, while 73 five-year-olds had failed to win it since See You Then performed the trick in 1985. It sounds persuasive but it's a bogus statistic because very few of the five-year-olds who had run were good enough to have a realistic chance of winning.

Katchit looked a few pounds below the best of his opponents, although he did have Alan King training him and Robert Thornton riding him, both of which were pluses.

King is everything a good jumps trainer should be. I think he's got as much determination as Nicholls, with less ego. Cheltenham brings out the best in King, and in Thornton, who has become the best Festival jockey there is.

Katchit's victory wasn't a great result for us because it sank our Jackpot, and something went wrong with Sizing Europe, who I'd backed to win almost £10,000. He started 2-1 favourite and finished tailed off.

Katchit is a solid, bombproof horse, but not a great one.

If this year's top four-year-old hurdlers, Celestial Halo and Franchoek, run in the 2009 Champion Hurdle, I'll have no qualms about backing either of them against Katchit. Next year, people won't be writing nonsense about five-year-olds being unable to win.

When it comes to people talking about horses' chances, Cheltenham is in a class of its own. Everyone does it. The word, whatever it is, spreads and seems to take on a life of its own. If you are not careful, you start listening.

We had backed An Accordion ante-post at 8-1 for the William Hill Chase and the previous day were contentedly imagining that we had got 8-1 about the 9-2 favourite. We had backed the likely winner and stolen the price. Good.

Then 50,000 people started talking about An Accordion and, by mid-morning, not only was his jumping suspect but he wasn't capable of clearing an obstacle. I thought he hadn't done much wrong when winning at Doncaster on his previous run, and the letters 'F' and 'U,' for 'fell' and 'unseated rider', didn't appear in his form at all. He was in form, he was trained by David Pipe, he was one of the most likely to improve, yet he drifted to 10.5 on Betfair.

When horses drift badly at a Monday meeting at Folkestone, there is usually a smelly rat to be found but this was a race at Cheltenham worth more than £50,000 to the winner. Connections weren't waiting for another day; this was the day, and An Accordion would definitely be trying, yet people had convinced themselves that he couldn't win. I had £333 on Betfair at 10.5 and, when An Accordion won, eventually at an SP of 7-1, I inevitably told myself that I should have had £666 or £888. There were certainly a lot of people asking themselves, why didn't I back that?

While they were asking themselves, one of JP McManus's horses, Garde Champetre, was winning the cross-country race. One of McManus's horses usually wins it. Some people like the cross-country race but I'm not one of them. As far as I'm concerned, it's a joke race that should be on It's A Knockout rather than at the Cheltenham Festival.

On the other hand, I'm all in favour of the closing race of the first day, the Fred Winter Juvenile Novices' Handicap Hurdle. It may take something away from the Triumph Hurdle but it's a terrific gambling race, full of horses people think may have been plotted up, with the Pipe yard running the winner of the previous weekend's Imperial Cup at Sandown, again. This time it was Ashkazar.

Since Ashkazar had beaten older horses impressively at Sandown, and was racing off the same handicap mark, he was a price that made every other horse, apart from River Liane, at least 12-1. River Liane, who was 11-4, had moved from France to Ireland and recently overwhelmed some decent older horses at Leopardstown.

In my column in the *Racing & Football Outlook* I'd tipped Crack Away Jack, but I didn't back it because, by the day of the race, I'd convinced myself that one or other of Ashkazar or River Liane would win. As 'hold-up' jockeys sometimes do, Paul Carberry rode a cracking race to win on Crack Away Jack, at 14-1. With our spread bet on cumulative SPs in mind, I didn't fully appreciate Carberry's skill, as he thoughtlessly plucked the race from Ashkazar's grasp.

That brought the first day's exploits to a reasonably successful conclusion, with An Accordion a good result and covering bets on Tidal Bay and Katchit. On the spread bets, SPs totalled just 49.5 while Noland was the only one of Nicholls' eight runners to have scored any points, five for finishing third in the Arkle Chase.

*

WEDNESDAY MARCH 12

For some reason, people think my role at Cheltenham is that of social secretary. Before Tuesday's cross-country race had been run, friends who were at the Festival for different reasons from me were already feeling thirsty and wanted to know what the arrangements were for the evening.

I left the course before Garde Champetre had passed the winning post but not to join them. My resolve was strong. In fact, it was a bit of a sad evening. I went back to Broadway and holed myself up in my hotel room. I had a bath, locked the door, turned my phone off and got to work on Wednesday's cards.

At 9pm I ventured into Broadway, had a quick pint in a fairly quiet pub, then had a lonely curry in the local Indian restaurant. Someone recognised me and said: 'I can't believe you've got no-one to eat with during Cheltenham week.'

I tried to convince him that it was by choice, but I'm not sure I succeeded.

I was in bed by 10.30pm, up at 5.30am and in the racecourse press room by 6.30am, with my laptop computer switched on, ready to go. When members of the Channel 4 Racing team arrived, they assumed that I had slept there. I've never been so well prepared for a day's racing. By 8am I was wondering what to do to fill the time, because I knew every race and every horse backwards. It felt fantastic.

Less encouragingly, news was filtering into my cocoon that it was very windy outside. Someone said that a roof had blown off the tented village and was flying towards Cleeve Hill. Brough Scott, Graham Cunningham and I soldiered on with a preview of the day's card on the *Racing Post* forum but we needn't have bothered because, at 8.30am, racing was abandoned, due to a hurricane.

Maintaining my resolve, I stuck it out until lunchtime, by which time I'd worked my way through most of Thursday's races. Then Simon Clare and David Stevens, Coral's representatives, said: 'That's it, we've had enough. Anyone want a lift into town?' I picked up my bags.

Evidently by 9.30am people were knocking on pub doors. I'm sure the publicans didn't mind too much. There were 20,000 punters with unspent gambling money burning a hole in their pockets. I walked into the Montpelier Wine Bar at about 1.30pm and thought to myself, I won't be coming out of here.

It's a great bar, and it was terrific fun. All the women working for the Tote had been sent home and they were in the bar, in their uniforms, drinking lager and smoking outside the door, as is their custom. I ended up talking to a woman who was a black witch, which prompted a lot of broomstick jokes. At 8pm we went for a Chinese meal and eventually ended up at the Queen's Hotel, although I'm pretty sure that Her Majesty wouldn't have been pleased to see me fly through the door. We then launched ourselves into the one-legged dancing competition, and things descended from there. By that time everyone was agreed that abandoning the second day of the Festival was an act of genius on the part of Edward Gillespie, Cheltenham's managing director, and should be repeated every year. They could race on Monday and Tuesday, take a break on Wednesday, then race again on Thursday and Friday.

*

THURSDAY MARCH 13

My head was fuzzy and I wasn't in the best physical or mental state for a ten-race marathon but I had already studied most of the races and managed to force myself through the remaining ones before presenting myself for another Betfair radio forum. I sat next to Mark Winstanley, who smelt as if he'd had a similar night to mine. As always with Mark, the bleep machine was going off regularly.

The afternoon got off to the best possible start. Old Benny, trained by Alan King, had always looked the type to come into his own over extreme distances and the four-mile National Hunt Chase was right up his street. I bought him for 11 on a 50-30-20-10 spread, then watched him travel notably well, and win by seven lengths. Then I took a bow to the crowd.

That was quickly followed by the Royal & SunAlliance Chase, an extremely weak one in which we'd backed Albertas Run ante-post at 16-1. I now had him priced up at 9-4, and he was available at 4-1. At the various Cheltenham previews, I seemed to be the only person in the country who thought that Albertas Run had beaten Air Force One fair and square in their previous outing in the Reynoldstown Chase at Ascot. Everyone else was saying that Albertas Run only won because of a fine ride by Ruby Walsh. Well, Tony McCoy was a fairly good replacement and although Jonjo O'Neill is a bit of an underachiever in terms of the horses he's trained, he had done nothing wrong with Albertas Run, who was running in the right race and only had to beat horses he had beaten before. Sometimes people try too hard to find reasons why a favourite won't win.

When you have backed a horse ante-post at long odds, it makes you reluctant to back it again at a much shorter price but if, on the day of the race, I think it's a 9-4 chance and I can get 4-1, I should back it again, which is what I did. We'd had £200 at 16-1 and I had another £800 at 4-1.

Whether he is riding at Cheltenham, or at Fontwell or Plumpton, McCoy tends to kick on down the final hill. He likes to make a decisive move early and, with his terrific upper body strength driving on, it isn't easy to get past McCoy's mount if he's established a lead. That's what he did on Albertas Run, and for me it was the easiest race to watch during the whole Festival.

I know something about the best Irish jockeys but I can't pretend to know what the form of a lot of the Irish horses represents. When I'm doing my tissue for a race, I tend to price the Irish runners up by reference to Betfair, but I did think Finger Onthe Pulse was a horse to take on in the Jewson Chase because in his last six starts Tom Taaffe's horse had fallen twice and been unseated once. Although I'm incapable of backing a winner ridden by Mark Bradburne, I backed his mount, Possol, at 25-1. Possol kept making mistakes but still managed to finish third, and I think he'll be a handicap chaser to follow next season. Two places in front of him was Finger Onthe Pulse.

When Master Minded won the Champion Chase, I witnessed one of the greatest chasing performances I have ever seen. It was breathtaking, with last year's winner, Voy Por Ustedes, struggling from a long way out to keep up and the others never getting into the race at all. Today, Master Minded was a monster of a horse.

I didn't get involved because, at various times during the run-up to the race, I fancied each of the four horses who had a chance of winning – Master Minded, Voy Por Ustedes, Twist Magic and Tamarinbleu. When that happens, you have to stand back.

There were still another six races to go and I'm glad I didn't back Mossbank in the next one, the Ryanair Chase, because if I had I'd have been seriously upset by the ride Davy Russell

gave him. Mossbank was always travelling well but Russell
didn't press the button soon enough. Maybe he thought that
Our Vic would either idle in front or not get home. There
were certainly plenty of people convinced that Our Vic
wouldn't win, and that he probably didn't want to. I looked
back at his races over the past two years and couldn't find
one in which Our Vic had run badly. He'd won nine times,
including twice over the course and distance. The race was
tailor-made for him and, in my book, he was favourite. In the
official book, he was 4-1 joint second favourite.

That was a winner for us, and so was Inglis Drever in the
World Hurdle. My policy with trainer Howard Johnson's
horses is to ignore everything he says about them. I think
he's a bit mischievous with the press. In his defence, I've
always found it amazing that trainers open up as much as
they do to journalists asking questions about their horses.
We expect an awful lot of them. I know trainers have a
responsibility to help promote the sport but they also have a
responsibility to their owners, who pay the bills. The mystery
and gamesmanship, the knowing a bit more than the man
next to you knows is part of the sport. I think anyone who
believes what some trainers tell them is mad, and any trainer
who tells everyone the truth is equally mad.

Different trainers behave very differently. Years ago, at the
start of a jumps season, I interviewed Paul Nicholls. After 40
minutes on the phone I had been given the winner of every
race at Cheltenham. Then I interviewed Martin Pipe. I was
on the phone for twice as long but when I put the phone

down I realised that I hadn't learnt anything at all about any of his horses, apart from the fact that they were all very nice and Pipe would have to consider where to run them. Trainers like Martin Pipe and Jonjo O'Neill could phone themselves up and not believe what they were hearing.

It wouldn't have happened in the old days. I can imagine a journalist phoning Ryan Price, a legendary, formidable figure who was champion jumps trainer five times, and asking if it was all right to visit his yard and be told all about Price's horses. Anyone getting within 200 yards of the horses would have been greeted by a pack of dogs and Price's shotgun. In some ways I think that's how it should be.

Our good run came to a jolting end when Mister McGoldrick, amazingly, romped home in the *Racing Post* Plate, at 66-1. That blew a hole in our SP spread bet, sank my bet on Gwanako, who finished second, and created a sore patch on my head, from scratching it. However many goes I was given, I still wouldn't have found Mister McGoldrick. How could an 11-year-old, the most exposed horse in the field, having his 68th race, turn a competitive handicap into a procession? There was no point even trying to work it out. The only saving grace was that the winner's SP might easily have been 100-1. He was that price on some boards in the ring and was trading at 130 on Betfair.

By the time Cousin Vinny won the Champion Bumper, at 12-1, it was just a matter of how bad the SP total would be, although our biggest bets had been on the earlier races, and they made it a good day overall.

I never have a bet in the bumper. It's not my kind of race. When half the field have a Timeform 'p' next to their name, indicating that they are likely to improve, it's time to leave well alone. While the Mullins family were celebrating Cousin Vinny's success, I was on my way to the Montpelier Wine Bar, to celebrate ours. At Cheltenham, there isn't much variation on the theme. It's usually the Montpelier.

The witch from the previous night was there again, along with a few more broomstick jokes. As far as I remember, I was reasonably well behaved until about 8pm, then things descended into the usual debauchery. Somehow I managed to get back to my hotel, to pay for the room I hadn't used. I still felt pretty perky, because we were about £25,000 up, which was roughly in line with our target.

The Festival provides some of the season's best betting opportunities. In most of the races there, I feel I can bet with a greater degree of confidence than elsewhere. We risk a lot of money and, if it goes wrong at Cheltenham, it will be difficult to recover. You need to be on your game. After two nights at the Montpelier, I probably wasn't.

*

FRIDAY MARCH 14

It has to be admitted that not as much homework was done for the Festival's final day, a nine-race epic. In a few races, I had already formed an opinion, and in a few more I wasn't going to be forming one.

The first race, the David Nicholson Mares' Hurdle,

certainly cleared my head but it almost emptied my stomach. I had just started a telephone tipping service and had put up Refinement as my bet of the day. Blinkered, as usual, I knew exactly what would happen to her. She is a mare who either has no respect for the hurdles, or is just clumsy, and doesn't seem to care. On top of that, she's lazy. If she had fingers, she'd enjoy sticking two of them up at Tony McCoy until he was provoked into applying the big stick although, nowadays, the stick isn't very big, or very firm. Eventually, Refinement would respond.

She eventually did and, five yards from the line, McCoy had forced her to the brink of victory. It would have been the ride of the meeting. Then, on the line, she stopped, and was beaten a short head by Whiteoak. Refinement was 10-1 and, to rub salt into the painful wound, Whiteoak was 20-1. Another nail in the SP coffin.

In the following race, the Ballymore Properties Novices' Hurdle, I backed Venalmar, who started at 11-1 and was beaten a neck by Fiveforthree. It wasn't as knife-edge as the previous finish but it was enough to make me squeal, which I don't often do, 'Oh no, not again!'

Instead of winning £15,000, I'd lost £1,500. I felt the gambling gods were against me. You know how it is, with those gods.

And so to the Coral Cup. When I analysed the race the day before, the horses I put at the top of the market were at the top of the market, which happens quite often in handicaps at the Festival. One of them was Junior, who had moved from

Brian Meehan's Flat yard to Alan King's largely jumps yard. In my book, any horse that goes from Meehan to King must have more than half a chance of improving. Junior finished third, at 12-1.

The winner was another near the top of my tissue, Naiad Du Misselot, trained by Ferdy Murphy. Murphy has been very successful at the Festival. Without having anything like the firepower of the leading stables, he'd had seven Festival winners over the years, including two long-priced ones in 2006 – You're Special and Hot Weld, both at 33-1 – and another brace in 2007, Joes Edge at 50-1 and L'Antartique at 20-1. Murphy was clearly very good at identifying horses capable of winning at Cheltenham, and getting them there fit to succeed. There was nothing wrong with Naiad Du Misselot's chance of winning, except his price. The bookmakers were scared of Murphy, understandably, and Naiad Du Misselot was 7-1, which was too short in my book.

Things were better on the price front in the Triumph Hurdle, thanks to Mark and I having backed Franchoek and Celestial Halo ante-post, the former at prices from 20-1 down to 9-2 and the latter at 10-1. It was pleasing to see them fight it out, although, to be greedy, we'd have preferred it if Franchoek had prevailed.

Mark and I both thought it was a quality race and we were surprised that Celestial Halo was offered at 14-1 for next year's Champion Hurdle afterwards, and Franchoek at 20-1. We have backed both of them. There could be another changing of the guard next year. Katchit is a grand horse but not a great one; Osana, who finished second, is said to be going chasing; Harchibald can no longer be regarded as a serious contender, and Sizing Europe may have a physical problem. A lot of people obviously don't agree, because Celestial Halo is now available at 20-1 and Franchoek at 33-1!

I hope the outcome isn't going to be the same as it was with Exotic Dancer in the Gold Cup. I fell into the trap of thinking that he was good value each-way and backed him some time ago. As it turned out, he wasn't good value and, if Master Minded was one of the best performances I've seen at Cheltenham, that of Denman was another. It was a spectacular, thrilling display, and I think Sam Thomas rode a terrific race. As they passed the stands for the first time he let out a bit of rein and, without seeming to quicken, Denman was suddenly a long way in front and not going to be beaten. There were some good horses behind him and they were totally out of contention a long way from the finish. It certainly wasn't a difficult race for the commentator.

Clive Smith, who owns Kauto Star, the runner-up in the Gold Cup, as well as Master Minded, is a very competitive man. I wonder if the decision to run Kauto Star at Aintree was influenced by a desire to see Kauto Star end the season on a high note. There will be horses who run well at both Cheltenham and Aintree but I thought Kauto Star would be vulnerable if he ran at Aintree. In the event, he did, and Our Vic just beat him.

Kauto Star was odds-on favourite in the Gold Cup and one of four favourites to finish second on Cheltenham's final day. With our spread bets on favourites and SPs in mind, it would have been nice if at least one of them had won, particularly Psycho, 5-1 favourite for the County Hurdle.

Considering the number of runners, 22, the race was slowly run, more slowly than the Triumph Hurdle. The crowd were certainly aware that Paul Carberry had Psycho at the back of the field in a race where the pace was steady but Carberry seemed less aware. He overdid the waiting tactics, made his move too late, and couldn't get to Silver Jaro, who held on at a crushing, for us, 50-1. The SPs made up to a grand, numbing total of 341.65. Ow! If only another hurricane had arrived after the Gold Cup.

I'd arranged to stay overnight in Cheltenham and then go on to Uttoxeter, where there was going to be a big Jackpot rollover. The friends I was staying with were soldiering on at the bar but the final two hours at the racecourse had taken the wind out of my sails. I was tired, and slightly pissed off. It felt as if the toast had kept falling butter-side down. I did a disappearing act and went home, feeling that it was not a case of a job well done.

When we added it all up, and subtracted it, we'd made a profit over the meeting of £10,000, although it didn't feel like it.

£10,000 isn't enough for the Cheltenham Festival, and the last day was a kick in the teeth, but to look on the bright side, how else could I make £2,500 a day or, with Wednesday's abandonment, £3,333 a day? I'm not knocking it but next year I think I'll change my approach.

I don't think I'll do the spread markets on SPs and favourites, selling SPs and buying favourites. I am not yet willing to concede that my theories are wrong, although the fact that I've had to write cheques out seems to suggest that they are. I still think that, now that it is a four-day meeting, there is a core of horses who can win while the rest can't. Admittedly, the evidence of the past two years makes it a difficult case to argue. At least we were right about Paul Nicholls' horses in handicaps. I'll be looking to oppose them again next year.

CHAPTER TWO

HOW I DO IT

Some readers of my previous book, *A Bloody Good Winner*, told me that they would like to know more about the way I work out a tissue for each race, the tissue being my list of prices for the runners, based on my opinion of each horse's chance of winning.

Making a tissue is something very few punters do but is at the heart of my approach, and the foundation of my success. If I didn't do my own tissues, I wouldn't have survived as a professional gambler for 15 years.

What most punters do is look at a race and try to find the winner. I think that is a quick and certain way of losing money because it doesn't take sufficient account of whether or not the horse you select represents good value at the available odds. Having chosen a horse the temptation, difficult to resist, is to back it almost regardless of its price, because we all know how frustrating it is to have picked the winner but not backed it. The trouble is, if you keep backing horses at 5-4 when their actual chance of winning is 7-4, although you will back plenty of winners, you will end up broke.

Instead of focusing on picking the winner, I focus on identifying horses who have a better chance of winnng than the available odds suggest. I am searching for that elusive goal, value.

For me, the starting point is the principle that every horse has a chance of winning the race being studied, simply by virtue of the fact that it is taking part. My job is to apply my knowledge of the form to the particular circumstances of the race in order to put a figure next to each horse, expressing its chance of winning. The figure is the price I consider to be an accurate reflection of its chance, whether 6-4 on or 25-1 against.

In a six-horse race, if each horse has an equal chance of winning, then each horse has a one in six chance, which can be expressed as odds of 5-1 against. In percentage terms, each of the six horses has a 16.67 per cent chance of winning, 100 per cent divided by six. Every price can be expressed as a percentage, so that odds of 8-1 represent an 11.11 per cent chance of winning (100 ÷ 9) while odds of 6-4, in other words 1.5-1, equate to a 40 per cent chance of winning (100 ÷ 2.5).

Here is a table laying out the percentages for all the different odds. Eventually, when you have done enough tissues, you won't need to refer to it because the figures will be in your head.

BETTING PERCENTAGES		
Odds on	**Price**	**Odds against**
50.00	Evens	50.00
52.38	11-10	47.62
54.55	6-5	45.45
55.56	5-4	44.44
57.89	11-8	42.11
60.00	6-4	40.00
61.90	13-8	38.10
63.64	7-4	36.36
65.22	15-8	34.78
66.67	2-1	33.33
69.23	9-4	30.77
71.43	5-2	28.57
73.33	11-4	26.67
75.00	3-1	25.00
76.92	100-30	23.08
77.78	7-2	22.22
80.00	4-1	20.00
81.82	9-2	18.18
83.33	5-1	16.67
84.62	11-2	15.38
85.71	6-1	14.29
86.67	13-2	13.33
87.50	7-1	12.50
88.89	8-1	11.31
90.00	9-1	10.00
90.91	10-1	9.09
92.31	12-1	7.69
93.33	14-1	6.67
94.12	16-1	5.88
95.24	20-1	4.76
96.15	25-1	3.85
97.06	33-1	2.94
97.56	40-1	2.44
98.04	50-1	1.96

When each horse's chance of winning is added together, the total for all the runners will be 100 per cent. The odds on a racecourse bookmaker's board, and in a betting shop, will add up to more than 100 per cent because the bookmaker needs to add a profit margin. In the earlier example, where each horse in a six-horse field has an equal chance of winning and the odds against each horse winning are therefore 5-1, the bookmaker might price all of the horses at 9-2, equivalent to 18.18 per cent per horse, making a total of 109 per cent. He might be greedier, or needier, and offer odds of only 4-1 against each horse, equivalent to 20 per cent per runner and 120 per cent in total. If a punter believes that the true odds against a particular horse winning are 3-1, it may still be worthwhile backing the horse at 4-1 but the size of the bookmaker's profit margin, albeit a theoretical one, is important, making it more or less difficult for a punter to win money. Knowing when the margins are against you, or in your favour, is very important. Most punters don't know. They would have a better chance of knowing if they did a tissue.

When I sit down to study a race and draw up a tissue, my aim is to produce a list of odds that provide as accurate an assessment as possible of the true chances of each horse winning the race. One of the advantages of 48-hour declarations is that the runners are printed in the *Racing Post* without a betting forecast. That saves me from the temptation to look at what the *Racing Post*'s predicted prices are, which is likely to influence my own prices.

Doing your own tissue is an excellent discipline although, of course, it is only as good as the compiler. You need to have a sound knowledge of the form, and of the various factors to be taken into account when assessing a horse's chance, in order to produce a list of prices sound enough to be useful.

Even if you have a good grasp of the form, your initial attempts at constructing a tissue are likely to produce some laughable results, with the total percentage way over 100 per cent and some odds completely different from those in the *Racing Post*'s betting forecast.

Remember, you are not trying to predict what the odds on offer will be but to give your opinion of each horse's actual chance of winning.

If, when you first try to construct a tissue, you put evens next to a horse's name, because you strongly fancy it to win, I'd be prepared to bet that, when you've priced up all the other horses, and add up the percentages, the grand total will be more than 100 per cent. Evens translates into 50 per cent, which means that the prices you put next to all the other horses must total only another 50 per cent. When they don't, and the grand total is, say, 125 per cent, you have to do something about it, either make the even money horse a 6-4 chance and slightly push out the other prices, or keep your favourite at evens and push some others out a lot. One way or another, you have to arrive at a total of 100 per cent.

Along the way, you will sometimes have a horse at 6-1 who the *Racing Post*'s betting forecast or a bookmaker's odds compiler has at 20-1. It doesn't necessarily mean that you are wrong but you need to look at the horse again to try to explain the discrepancy. Either you have missed something, or you have found the best bet of the week.

It takes time but doing your own tissue is an excellent discipline, an education that will give you a better feel for the relationship between odds and chances, and a better understanding of margins and the way markets work.

The way to make money is not to try to find the winner of every race but to get the percentages in your favour. Backing horses at 5-4 when their actual chance of winning is 7-4 is, indeed, a quick way to the workhouse but, to look on the bright side, backing horses at 7-4 when they should be 5-4 is an equally quick way to a fortune.

I sit down with John Whitley's ratings and the *Racing Post* website on the screen, for the form, and expect to have produced a tissue for a single race in about 30 minutes. I have learnt that, if it takes much longer, I am probably no better off than when I started and if my initial attempt produces a total of 80 per cent rather than 100 per cent, it means it's a race that I don't think will have a winner. I must have gone down the list of runners putting 12-1 next to most of them, either because they are all useless or because they have run against each other so often that there is no angle, nothing to make me feel that one has an edge over another.

One of the problems is staying on top of the form, which has become increasingly difficult. There were over 1,400 more races in 2007 than in 1997, and I was ten years older, with more work commitments. As a result, I've found myself paying less attention to the worst races, full of less reliable horses, and more to the better ones. I sometimes think that, if I lived in Scotland, I might end up concentrating on the horses who race at the Scottish tracks. It would be another way of focusing on a limited number of races.

For me, the easiest races to price up are the heritage handicaps for older horses because they are full of horses I know well, with an established pattern to their form. I know each horse's ability and the circumstances in which it performs best, and worst, and can apply that knowledge to the particular circumstances of the race, such as the track, going and draw.

Normally, I am looking for a weakness in a favourite, although you have to be careful not to be looking with too much determination, or you end up opposing favourites simply because they are favourites. The price you allot the favourite in your tissue helps to determine the prices of the rest of the field, because it dictates what percentage all the other runners must total to arrive at 100 per cent.

The races that excite me most are the ones where I believe the first two in the betting have holes in them. If I think the next two or three horses in the betting have at least as much chance as the front two, I feel confident of making a profit. Ideally, I like to see a horse I have put in at 9-2 available at 8-1. It is probably 9-2 with me and 8-1 with the bookmakers because the market thinks the favourite has a better chance of winning than I do, and has it at a shorter price than I have.

It is about trying to get the percentages in your favour. You can get them in your favour by identifying horses who you don't think can win. Where a horse has no chance, and is probably available at massive but still unappealing odds on Betfair, I put a cross by it and count it as 0 per cent in my tissue. If you cross a horse out, then look at the betting forecast and see that it is expected to be 7-1, it means that you have crossed out 12.5 per cent, which means that you have pretty much taken out the bookmakers' profit margin. Of course, that isn't going to do you much good if you keep crossing out 7-1 shots that win about one time in eight. Your judgement has got to be right.

Another way of looking at it is that, on Betfair, the odds for a race will total about 102 per cent, which means that in theory, to break even, you have to beat the market by two per cent plus whatever percentage commission you are paying to Betfair on your winnings. If you have identified two 20-1 shots who you think cannot win, knocking them out is equivalent to knocking out 9.52 per cent (4.76 per cent x 2), which means that the percentages are now in your favour.

Gradually, you will get to know when you are right and have confidence in your opinion. I do a tissue every day but I don't stick to it religiously because circumstances change in the run-up to the race. The going may change, or you may see something you like or dislike about a horse in the parade ring, or you may see someone who you only ever see at the racecourse when a particular stable is running a fancied horse.

In 1990, Mark Coton wrote a book called *Value Betting*. Really, the subject can be summarised in one sentence. You can make a profit by backing horses who are available at better odds than their chance of winning. The difficulty is knowing what their true chance of winning is. My life as a professional gambler is based on knowing that more accurately than the market.

I work on the basis of a 15 per cent margin of error in my assessment of a horse's chance of winning. If I can back a horse at a price more than 15 per cent better than the price I think it should be, then I will back it. Sometimes, I will back two or three horses in the same race. I suggest you try doing the same. If, after having given it a decent go, you find that you are losing money, maybe you should do something else; the National Lottery, perhaps.

CHAPTER THREE

AINTREE TALES

It is so easy to preach about gambling, and so hard to practice what you preach. I pray regularly that I will not be given inside information because it is so seductive and usually useless. Please don't tell me what you know and, if you do, please give me the strength to ignore it.

On Saturday March 29 I was on a train to Doncaster. It was the opening day of the Flat season, in as far as it has got one – Lincoln day. Someone close to Peter Chapple-Hyam told me that two of his horses were absolute certainties. My informant informed me that the trainer himself was going to back them.

First of all, by the time this sort of nugget of information has reached me, it's probably already reached 50 other people. Second, I've never met a trainer, even a good trainer, who has really prospered from backing his own horses. Such trainers may exist, they may not. If they do, they are probably an endangered species, like orangutans. Third, the information is often wrong or, if it's right, doesn't help.

The certainties were running in two divisions of a seven-furlong maiden race for three-year-olds. The first was Brave Prospector. When I saw him in the parade ring I wasn't impressed. He didn't look like a horse who had thrived during the winter. On the other hand, his opponents didn't have much in the way of form while, as a two-year-old, Brave Prospector had finished fourth in a Group 3 race, albeit one of dubious quality, and was rated 101. Chapple-Hyam's stable had made a good start to the season, so I thought I'd go with it. Brave Prospector started at 8-15 on and finished ninth of 12.

The other horse was Onceaponatime. I'd been advised to take an early price, so I squeezed all the 5-2 I could out of it, then watched it drift to 4-1. It was the last race of the day. The sky was black and the rain was freezing, and I was in Doncaster. It can't get much worse than that. Onceaponatime did a bit better than Brave Prospector, finishing eighth of 12. I stood in the rain, waiting for a taxi, and asked myself, what have you done?

What I'd done was break one of my own rules, the one that says, don't pay attention to inside information. Sometimes it will be a help but most of the time it won't. I know that I am better off relying on my own knowledge and observations. I suppose it is good to succumb to the temptation occasionally because it puts you on your guard for a while. Unfortunately, learning your lesson involves losing money. Onceaponatime won his next two races while Brave Prospector subsequently won a valuable sprint handicap at York, but that didn't help me.

I love the Lincoln but the Flat season doesn't really start until the Craven meeting at Newmarket in mid-April and, after Cheltenham, everyone is looking towards Aintree.

It was at Aintree that I met 'the nigger with the trigger', the result of a losing day at the races followed by a drinking evening in Liverpool. The meeting had its origins several months earlier, in a different part of the country.

I had been putting bets on for a big punter. When the minus figure reached £86,000, I called a stop and told him I wouldn't put on any more bets for him until he had paid me. He told me I could go and collect the money from him. It was a long way to go but, for £86,000, it was worth it. When I asked for directions, he told me to phone him when I'd arrived in the vicinity, and he'd give me directions then.

When I arrived, and phoned, he told me to look out of the car window. 'You'll see a big house with big gates.' He was right. I didn't have any trouble getting through the gates but I was a bit worried about getting back out again.

When I reached the house, it was guarded by a huge dog on a chain. The dog looked as if he was taking a break from guarding the gates of Mordor, in *The Lord of the Rings*. He was enormous. There was no way I was going to step out of the car to shake its paw, so I sat where I was, and hooted the horn. The man came out, escorted me in, made me a cup of coffee, and presented me with a carrier bag full of banknotes. I wasn't sure what £86,000 in readies looked like, so I asked, 'Is this all of it?'

'No,' he said. 'That's half of it. If you ever ask me for the other half, I'll kill you.'

At that moment, half the money and the ability to carry on breathing seemed like a reasonable deal, so I accepted it, got back in the car and drove off, fast, to Fontwell.

I was convinced that someone would be waiting to ambush me; that every car that appeared in my rear view mirror had been dispatched to recover the money. Fortunately, I arrived safely at Fontwell, the bag of money still in the boot.

Occasionally, I'd think about the remaining £43,000 and what I could do with it. At the end of the indulgent evening in Liverpool, I was feeling a bit morose and, slumped in a chair, told a big guy who I had struck up a conversation with the sad tale of the missing money. He put an enormous arm round my shoulder and said: 'Don't worry. I can get that money for you. That's what I do. I usually charge 35 per cent. Just leave it to me. They call me "the nigger with the trigger".'

I quickly sobered up and told myself not to make things worse. 'No, it's alright,' I said, 'I'll leave it be.' Mercifully, I haven't heard from the punter or from the man with the trigger since.

*

AINTREE
THURSDAY APRIL 3

The prize-money at Aintree is so good nowadays that horses who run well at Cheltenham are more or less bound to run there. Everyone then spends their time wondering how they'll perform in comparison to Cheltenham.

There are various theories and a lot of pontificating and an awful lot of bollocks talked in the press room and the bars. The most bizarre theory I heard this year, and from a colleague I respect, was that a horse can't win at Aintree if it won at Cheltenham but if it finished second at Cheltenham, it could.

What sense is there in that? The fact that Inglis Drever, who won at Cheltenham, was beaten at Aintree while Binocular and Gwanako, who had been second at Cheltenham, won, doesn't prove the theory correct. The truth is that nobody knows how a horse will perform at Aintree when it has run at Cheltenham.

I kept studying Inglis Drever and wondering why he couldn't win again. There was no evidence that his opponents in the Liverpool Hurdle were more likely to be suited to Aintree than he was, and his Aintree record was better than people suggested. I ended up having six grand on him.

It seems that I was wrong. Inglis Drever finished third to Blazing Bailey, who he had beaten three times out of three during the season. Trainer Howard Johnson then said that Inglis Drever wasn't suited to the track.

That was the first race of the meeting, which didn't exactly get it off to a flying start. Then it was Kauto Star's turn, in the Totesport Bowl Chase. During previews for Aintree, I'd watched several replays of the Gold Cup and, each time I watched, Kauto Star looked more legless. Paul Nicholls was bullish about his chance but Nicholls is always bullish. Kauto Star would be odds-on but I thought he was ripe for laying and at 4-7 the downside was limited. I laid Kauto Star and backed Our Vic and Gungadu.

It turned out to be the luckiest race of the season for me because if Kauto Star hadn't ploughed through the second last fence, he'd have won. It was a credit to Nicholls that

Kauto Star showed no serious ill effects from the hard race he'd had at Cheltenham. He is still a very good horse but he ran below his best at both Cheltenham and Aintree, and his jumping can still cause problems. A French-bred eight-year-old, Kauto Star's best performances are probably behind him.

After the Triumph Hurdle, I backed Celestial Halo and Franchoek for next year's Champion Hurdle but after watching Binocular trounce Celestial Halo in the novices' hurdle at Aintree, I now think he will beat both of them, and win it. I don't agree with people who think Binocular has a long way to go before he matches Katchit. Binocular ran a cracking race against older horses in the Supreme Novices' Hurdle, finishing second to Captain Cee Bee in a time significantly faster than the Champion Hurdle, and his jumping was much better at Aintree. I haven't backed Binocular for the Champion Hurdle yet because I don't think his current price, 7-1, will change much for quite a while.

In *A Bloody Good Winner*, I wrote 'spread betting firms have got no chance against me. They can't beat me, and I can't see how they ever will'. Sporting Index obviously agree, because they closed my account a long time ago, leading to a game of hide-and-seek as I try to get my bets on through other people while Sporting Index try to spot them. If I carry on selling SPs, as I did at Aintree as well as Cheltenham, they may soon offer to accommodate me. I will need accommodating, because Sporting Index will have my house.

I sold SPs on the opening day and after Christy Beamish had won the Fox Hunters' Chase at 6-1, bringing the total winners' SPs for the first four races to 21.4, I thought we had nothing to worry about. Then Stan won the Red Rum Handicap Chase at 25-1.

That wasn't too bad because I backed Stan, at 40-1, although not for a lot. He had run well in the same race at 33-1 the previous year and was ridden by Aidan Coleman, who is good value for his 5lb allowance. The race was just a glorified Worcester handicap.

After Elusive Dream won the penultimate race at 7-2 I set off for the hotel where I caught the final bit of the commentary on the last race on the telephone. The commentator was saying: 'and what price was that?' Only a few words, but they filled me with dread. The horse he was talking about was Auroras Encore, who had fallen in his last two races but didn't fall in this one. Instead, he won at 50-1. We had sold the SPs at 58 and they had made up to 99.9.

Staying at Liverpool's Stalag Hotel didn't make me feel any better, and I sacked the person who found it for me, in a bargain bucket on the internet. To be fair, the hotel was perfect if you had just carried out a robbery and needed to make a quick exit onto the nearby motorway. Otherwise, it wasn't. Even Alan Partridge might have committed suicide there.

Unsurprisingly, there was a constant stream of taxis taking guests elsewhere. A group of us got into a cab, a Skoda of dubious vintage, and set off for the bright lights of Liverpool.

When I asked the driver where the winder for the window was, he told me that someone had nicked it. We asked him what it was like living in Liverpool and he said it was murder, literally. He kept pointing at local landmarks. 'See that place there? That's where that young kid got shot, just over there . . . That pub, that's where I got shot and, see that? That's where my mate got stabbed.' By the time we reached the city centre I was almost too scared to get out of the cab and go to a cashpoint.

We went to a restaurant called Jellons, which was very good. Possibly because some of the girls there had very little on, several fellow diners decided to go on to a place called X in the City. It's what I think is known as a gentlemen's club, and boasts the largest lap dancing bar in Liverpool. Basically, it takes all the guesswork out of it, and every jockey, trainer and stable lad that you never want to meet is there. On this occasion, I gave it a miss.

*

FRIDAY APRIL 4

We'd done the Jackpot on Thursday and had all six winners – but not all in the same line. The Jackpot wasn't won and, by the time the first race was run on Friday, the pool contained almost £720,000. We had another go, with perms totalling £9,500. That is a massive perm, at least for Mark and me, but to provide good cover in the most difficult races still pushes you towards having a banker somewhere. If you increase the number of selections in a race from, say, six to seven, you only increase the total cost by 16.7 per cent but if you have two selections instead of one in a race, the cost doubles.

We had five winners and the 2-5 favourite, Master Minded, as a banker in the Melling Chase. When he was beaten, it was gut-wrenching. In the final race, the two remaining tickets in the 17-runner Totepool Handicap Chase were on Boychuk and Oedipe. Oedipe won, at 20-1, and someone who had only bet £32 on the Jackpot scooped £511,000.

Apart from that, as Abraham Lincoln's wife may have said after their theatre outing, it was a good day.

In the opening Mildmay Novices' Chase I had decent each-way bets on Roll Along and Big Buck's. I thought Roll Along had been held up for too long when second to Albertas Run in the Royal & SunAlliance Chase at Cheltenham, and was great value at 8-1, and I thought Big Buck's had been campaigned over trips too short for him and would improve for the step up to beyond three miles. In the Jewson Chase at Cheltenham, over two and a half miles, he had been hampered and blundered but still stayed on strongly. The horse I couldn't have was Battlecry, who had a hard race at Cheltenham and had been doing the donkey work all season. I was wrong about him; he ran a good race to be second – to Big Buck's.

After that, I fell for Tazbar, favourite for the Sefton Novices' Hurdle. Keith Reveley's horse had won three novice hurdles impressively and, through various form lines, had the beating of just about every other horse in the race. I thought, this is the real thing, and had £4,000 on it. I also backed Pettifour, who won at 16-1, but only recovered half what I staked on Tazbar.

When Mary Reveley, Keith's mother, was training, she was reluctant to run horses at the Cheltenham Festival, and Keith seems to be the same. Having watched Tazbar's performance at Aintree, I think Reveley made the wrong decision. He chose a speed track when Tazbar strikes me as more of an Inglis Drever type, suited by a testing track. If Reveley is prepared to run Tazbar at Cheltenham next year, I think he could become a legitimate contender for the World Hurdle, although he will have to improve.

Then came the pain of Master Minded. When he won the Champion Chase at Cheltenham, beating Voy Por Ustedes by 19 lengths, he looked as if he would stay two and a half miles, but he didn't. Voy Por Ustedes beat him by 18 lengths. Least said, soonest forgotten.

Ruby Walsh is the best jockey there is over the Grand National fences, terrific to watch and in a league of his own. Gwanako, who had finished second in the *Racing Post* Plate at Cheltenham, was a rare example, for the time of year, of an unexposed Paul Nicholls-trained horse. There were 29 runners but very few with good chances. I backed Nacarat, who was undone by an over-exuberant jump, and Gwanako, who jumped like a cat and seemed to have the race won a long way out, until Irish Raptor almost got back up again. Fortunately for me, he didn't.

It was Nicholls and Walsh again in the next race, won by Pierrot Lunaire, at 5-1. I had £1,500 each-way on both the winner and Greenbridge, who was unplaced. The Jackpot hurt but otherwise Friday was a good day. The night was less exciting. I never managed to escape from Hotel Stalag.

At least it meant I made a good start on studying Saturday's card and had time to go to the gym and get into some sort of training for the London Marathon, in nine days' time. I must be mad.

*

SATURDAY APRIL 5

Grand National day didn't get off to a great start. Overnight, I was definitely going to back Pearl King, owned by JP McManus, famed for his punting exploits. Pearl King drifted on Betfair while Song Of Songs, also owned by JP McManus, was backed. I was suckered into thinking that the McManus team preferred the chances of Song Of Songs, and backed that, instead. Song Of Songs was pulled up while Pearl King romped home, at 10-1. I don't want to hear anyone saying the game is easy. It isn't easy, it's horribly difficult, and exasperating.

I get exasperated with myself sometimes. Tidal Bay was 6-4 favourite for the Maghull Novices' Chase, and he was entitled to be. He had won the Arkle Chase at Cheltenham as if he was another Arkle, jumping fantastically, had much the best form and was running in a less competitive race. If you were having £4,000 on each day's banker, Tidal Bay was definitely the day's £4,000 bet. All I had on it was £1,000, although I did also buy Tidal Bay in a match bet with Takeroc, the 5-2 second favourite. Why didn't I have more? Partly because I find it difficult to have a lot on a short-priced horse, even though a short-priced horse can represent good value, and partly because I'd read Paul Nicholls' column in the *Racing Post*, in which he'd extolled the virtues of Takeroc.

There is a saying in the City, 'people buy the rumour and sell the facts'. The facts were that Tidal Bay had proved himself to be top class whereas, in England, Takeroc had only looked very promising when winning a four-horse race at Sandown, having won four jumps races at Pau. He was an unknown quantity who Nicholls thought highly of and might turn out to be very good. He would have to be to beat Tidal Bay. He didn't, although Takeroc ran well to be beaten six lengths.

In the Aintree Hurdle I got it wrong, took the view that Osana would be too good for Al Eile, despite the latter's very good record at the course, and suffered accordingly. Things soon looked up again with my nap of the day, if not of the meeting, Forest Pennant, yet another winner for Nicholls and Walsh. Every time Forest Pennant ran, he looked as if he would improve over a longer trip, even though he was winning over shorter ones. When he was beaten at Sandown, a month before Aintree, I thought the race was one of the best handicap hurdles of the season. Now he was running over three miles against exposed horses. I had £4,000 each-way on Forest Pennant, £1,000 each-way at 13-2 and the rest at 5-1.

That was the highlight of National day for me. In the race that was more important to most people I backed Simon and D'Argent, who unseated their riders, Cloudy Lane, who finished sixth, and Comply Or Die, who won, eventually starting at 7-1. Then I set off home.

I have a theory that the races after the National don't actually exist, and I prefer not to hang around to find out. I won about £30,000 over the three days but left thinking that it was definitely getting harder. The margins were more difficult and, when I was losing, I was finding it more difficult to pick myself up.

CHAPTER FOUR

DIVING INTO DIFFERENT POOLS

What I discovered from running the London Marathon on April 13 was that I am too old, it is too far and I wasn't fit enough. None of which came as a surprise. I did it because my ego got the better of reason, again.

Twenty-five years ago, I had no trouble finishing the Sydney Marathon but, last year, aged 45, I found it a lot harder to finish the Brands Hatch half-marathon. I finished 487th, which should have told me something. Don't do it again and don't even think about doing a full marathon. I did.

During January and February the training gave me something useful to do but by the time the Cheltenham Festival arrived, it was all over. I had subscribed to a website that provided a daily training regime for marathon runners. It's fine if you are unemployed and can spare the 40 hours a week required but, otherwise, it's not. I suspect that all good marathon runners have got serious personal issues and have discovered that marathon training is the only way they can escape them. It keeps them out of the house for most of the daylight hours.

I didn't run every day but for a while I did go to the gym almost every day until I peaked with an 18-mile run from Tunbridge Wells to Sevenoaks. I walked the last two miles and felt totally demoralised. When Cheltenham's Wednesday card was abandoned I could have spent the day training but when everyone else was in the pub having a good time the idea of running up and down Cleeve Hill lacked allure. During Aintree, I did actually go to the gym once, which quite surprised me.

When I finally lined up in Greenwich Park, I was reasonably fit for a non-runner but hopelessly unfit for a marathon runner. Somehow, after 16 miles, I was still smiling, still running, and thinking, 'I've cracked it'. After 18 miles, I wanted to die. I was in a freezing hailstorm somewhere on the Isle of Dogs. I was staggering in one direction, the front of my thighs killing me, wanting to lie down, curl up and cry. Hurtling towards me in the opposite direction, having already conquered Canary Wharf, were the marathon fanatics, showing no signs of pain but looking as if they could do with a decent breakfast.

I didn't stop because I knew that, if I did, I'd never get started again. It was a reasonably flat course, following the Thames most of the way, but eventually the slightest incline felt horrific and, towards the end, going downhill hurt even more.

Martin Lel won, in two hours five minutes. I finished 21,969th, in five hours 35 minutes. At least I wasn't one of the 4,093 starters who needed medical assistance, including 40 who ended up in hospital. It was a relief to hear that no one had actually died because, if someone had, I think it might have been me.

That's it. My marathon days are over.

*

A few years ago were golden years for punters. Even before the arrival of betting exchanges, the betting market was becoming more competitive. The only way bookmakers could compete effectively was on price and, for five or six years, their margins fell to the point where knowledgeable punters could bet profitably. My knowledge of the form and of markets and staking was better than most other punters, so I thrived.

Betfair has been a huge boon but it has contributed to a change in the marketplace that is now making it more difficult for me to make a good living from betting.

The prices on Betfair are determined by many of the cleverest and most knowledgeable bettors in racing. As a result, they provide a very accurate guide to each horse's actual chance of winning. There is no longer any need for bookmakers to employ an odds compiler and far fewer of them bet to their own opinions than when I first turned professional, in 1993. It is no longer in a bookmaker's interest to do so. What they have to do, instead, is locate themselves in the best position possible for extracting money from punters, whether on course or off course. On course, the prices are pretty much all the same on all the bookmakers' boards, and all are dictated by Betfair. There is no point racegoers walking up and down the rows of bookmakers, searching out the best price. They may as well be kind to their feet, and go to the nearest pitch.

There are now far fewer discrepancies between my tissue prices and the prices available in the market. All the heroes who were once willing to lay a 12-1 shot at 33-1 have gone and the market for most races is very thin until close to the time of the race, when a huge amount of business is done.

Maybe I am past my sell-by date but I don't think so. I just think it has become harder, and I need to discover some fresh angles. An evening I spent with Harry Findlay in April made me think.

Harry has always been a fearless punter and as the colourful, outspoken joint-owner of Denman, the Hennessy and Cheltenham Gold Cup winner, he is now the best-known punter in Britain. I have always regarded him as an impending car crash, speeding along, going faster and faster, having bigger and bigger bets on odds-on chances until the wheels suddenly fall off. Now, I've changed my mind, not least because he is prospering more than I am, which suggests that he's got something right that I've missed.

When betting exchanges first arrived, I was seduced by the fact that 10-1 shots were suddenly available at 20-1. Failed punters who thought they could make easy money by laying horses were laying them at well over the odds. That was great while it lasted but those days are largely gone, and Harry was paying attention to the other end of the market, short-priced favourites.

Over the years, backers of odds-on favourites have been much maligned by the betting cognoscenti but the abolition of betting duty, bringing an end to bookmakers' deductions from punters' winnings, and the emergence of Betfair, with its smaller margins, suddenly made it much more attractive to back short-priced horses. At the same time, layers were tempted to lay short-priced favourites because they felt that, if they laid a 6-4 on shot, and it won, the damage wouldn't be great. In novice chases they fell into the trap of thinking, the favourite's got to jump all those fences, and they'd lay it at over the odds.

Harry's reaction was to up his game, and bet even bigger. He thinks nothing of having £60,000 or £100,000 on a horse at 6-4 on if he believes it should be 3-1 on. I remember a novice hurdler called Big Fella Thanks running at Taunton on January 29. A few weeks earlier it had won a similar race at Chepstow easily. Big Fella Thanks opened at 9-4 on, Harry piled on, and it won equally easily at 100-30 on. Harry or, strictly speaking, his mother Margaret, is a part-owner of Big Fella Thanks so Harry was well placed to know about the horse's wellbeing.

What Harry had done, through his own judgement and knowledge, was find an angle that gave him an edge in the market. That is how you get ahead of the game, and I don't suppose Harry minds running his own horses in bad races where the market will price them up at 5-4 on when he knows that their actual chance of winning is 4-1 on. If you are willing and able to risk a huge amount of money for relatively little gain, you can exploit the way the market has evolved to make, cumulatively, a lot of money.

I don't think there is anything wrong with Harry's approach, and talking to him made me think harder about how, in the future, I could put myself in a position that gave me a similar advantage. One possibility was the Tote, another was expanding my existing involvement in buying and managing horses.

Betfair is dominated by relatively sophisticated punters whereas the big pool bets operated by the Tote, notably the Jackpot, Placepot and Scoop6, are populated by less sophisticated punters. If you were being unkind, you could say that a lot of the Tote's customers were mug punters. It makes sense to bet against mug punters rather than against better informed ones, particularly when there is 'carryover' money in a pool.

On the face of it, the 29 per cent the Tote deducts from Jackpot pools (30 per cent from Scoop6 pools) is prohibitive but several bookmakers now offer cashback to big players. I get ten per cent of my stake back, which brings the percentage down to 119 per cent. If you regard this as a six-race bet, the percentage is just over three per cent per race, and there are some big carryovers.

Another advantage with pool bets is that you don't suffer the frustration of having people trying to get your bets on for you before the advertised price has disappeared. It is the same frustration with the tips I give on my telephone service. On March 27, I tipped a horse called Dovedale in a handicap hurdle at Exeter. In the morning, the best price advertised with fixed-odds firms was 12-1, with longer odds available on Betfair for small sums. By the time I managed to get on, the best price was 13-2 and Dovedale eventually won at 4-1. I don't blame the bookmakers for not wanting to lay substantial amounts at their morning prices but I imagine quite a few of my tipping service customers were running around, driving themselves mad, as I was, chasing the price. That is the nature of the beast.

Another reason Jackpot and Scoop6 bets are going to figure prominently in my betting this summer is that, if I am going to win hundreds of thousands of pounds, it will be by landing a big Jackpot or Scoop6. Personally, I wish they'd convert the Scoop6 into a Scoop7 because then there would be more big rollovers and people who invested the most time, money and knowledge would have a bigger advantage over other punters, which would suit me. Also, it might stop me having nightmares about Agnes Haddock, who won £410,322 for £2 on the Scoop6 in January 2007 by backing horses such as Clouding Over because that's what it was doing when she went into the betting shop. I don't know why she chose Whispered Secret in the final leg but I know I had the horses who finished second and third. The following Saturday, Agnes won the bonus, another £278,288.

I don't suppose I will get my wish, because the Tote don't want someone like me winning the Scoop6 and they certainly don't want someone like Harry Findlay winning it, although he still does.

So, Mark and I decided to focus more on the big pool bets. They are growing faster and bigger than in the past, which is good for the Tote and, on the face of it, good for me but I think the reason they are getting bigger, faster, is that they are attracting more clever money. As it has become harder to win money on Betfair, other knowledgeable punters have also decided that Jackpot and Scoop6 bets offer good value.

Mark and I spent a lot of time debating when we should and shouldn't get involved. There is an argument for staying out once the pool has more than about £400,000 in it because the big syndicates will then step in with huge perms. We can't compete with them and, if we did win, we would probably have to share the pot with winning tickets belonging to the big syndicates. Perhaps it is better to concentrate on much smaller pools of about £40,000, when we won't be playing against too much clever money, hopefully.

*

Focusing more on big pool bets was one way forward; another was focusing more on buying and managing racehorses. I have owned horses, wholly or in parts, for more than 20 years, and organised several syndicates. Our Heading for the Rocks partnership hit gold with Rising Cross, a small but tenacious filly who we bought for 20,000 euros and sold for £325,000 after she finished second in the 2006 Oaks. Rising Cross went on to finish third in the Irish Oaks before winning the Park Hill Stakes at York.

Most of the horses I was involved with won their fair share of races but at a modest level. I reached the conclusion that syndicates at the lower end of the market don't have much to offer financially either for the people in them, or for those who organise them or for the trainer. In future, I wanted to operate at a higher level.

More luck is involved in buying thoroughbreds than in backing them, as a long list of costly, beautifully bred but useless racehorses testifies. Even so, I think there is a realistic chance of making decent money, whereas the chances of making millions from betting are becoming less.

Last summer I thought the weakness of the dollar meant that there would be some good buys available at the sales in America. I discussed it with trainer John Best, who was finding it hard to buy the sort of yearlings he wanted, within our budget, at the Newmarket and Doncaster sales. Any horse with a good pedigree and looks to match was out of our price range and we didn't want to buy well-bred horses without the looks to match. Our only hope was to find horses with good conformation but relatively unattractive pedigrees, and hope that their looks weren't deceiving. John had already done well with horses bought cheaply through Anthony Bromley's and David Minton's Highflyer Bloodstock. As well as Rising Cross, Best had bought Kingsgate Native for 20,000 guineas. As a two-year-old, he had been narrowly beaten in both the Windsor Castle Stakes at Royal Ascot and the Molecomb Stakes at Goodwood, and subsequently won the Group 1 Nunthorpe Stakes at York before finishing second in the Group 1 Prix de l'Abbaye at Longchamp.

After the Nunthorpe several people phoned John and myself to say that they had liked the look of the horse at the sales but had been put off by its pedigree. John Mayne had given Best a certain amount to spend at the sales and he had bought Kingsgate Native for him.

Best and I decided to set up Kent Bloodstock with the idea of getting a small number of people to put up £100,000 each, to fund the purchase of better horses than previous partnerships had been able to buy. During the blaze of publicity following Kingsgate Native's triumph in the Nunthorpe, 15 people came forward with a definite 'yes'. By the time we had spent £700,000, and asked for the money, ten of them had disappeared.

The ones that came good did come good because, again through Highflyer Bloodstock, Best added to his record of success with cheaply bought horses. Kent Bloodstock's first collection included Mullionmileanhour and Deposer, bought at the Doncaster Sales in August 2007 for 26,000 guineas and 19,000 guineas respectively.

Best had another important new owner to buy for, Dave Gorton. By a stroke of luck, I knew Gorton from my time working in the City. Possibly because he didn't drink as many pints of lager as me, and is very clever, Gorton is now a leading hedge fund manager. Every year, I get invited to his box at Royal Ascot and, after Kingsgate Native came nail-bitingly close to winning the Windsor Castle Stakes, he said he would like to have a go. I was thrilled because I knew that, if Dave did get involved in owning horses, he'd want it to be at a level that gave him a realistic chance of having a horse good enough to win good races.

At Doncaster, we bought Flashmans Papers for Gorton, for 38,000 guineas. The previous week I went to Florida with Best, to the Fasig-Tipton Sales at Ocala and, in September, we went to the Keeneland Sales in Kentucky. It was exhilarating; I love auctions but, for me, it was very much a learning exercise. John knows horses while I just walk round them and nod sagely. I am trying to learn from him. At Ocala, the horses he bought for Gorton included Elegant Cad, for $80,000, and at Keeneland, through the Kern Lillingston Association bloodstock agency, Square Eddie, for $200,000. For 2008, Gorton would have two other two-year-olds, Yaldas Girl and Great Bounder.

Altogether, we bought about 40 foals and yearlings, many of whom have since been bought by Gorton, Kent Bloodstock and other patrons of Best's yard. I am managing Gorton's horses, with a mandate to provide him with runners at the big summer meetings he attends, particularly Royal Ascot and Glorious Goodwood. It is quite a challenge.

I have always wanted to be a racing manager because, as far as I can tell, as long as you know the programme book, it doesn't involve doing anything that could properly be described as work. On Racing UK, during the days leading up to the Craven meeting at Newmarket in April, someone remarked that it was going to be a very busy week for Teddy Beckett, now Lord Grimthorpe, Khalid Abdullah's racing manager, because he would have runners at both Newmarket and Newbury. I wondered what Lord Grimthorpe would be busy doing. Making sure the lobster was ready for lunch? Opening another bottle of champagne? Telling Abdullah that his horse had run well?

So far, I haven't had to tell Gorton that one of his horses has been injured on the gallops, which must be an unpleasant duty. In fact, so far, I haven't had to deliver any bad news at all, because none of his horses have run yet. When they do, I hope they run fast.

CHAPTER FIVE

APRIL DOWNPOURS

NEWMARKET
APRIL 17

The second day of the Craven meeting, and Dave Gorton's debut as a racehorse owner; my debut as a racing manager; Yaldas Girl's debut as a racehorse. At least two of us were apprehensive.

Gorton arrived in a helicopter with four of his City mates, barrow boy types, two of whom I knew. I'd booked them into the Champions' Gallery restaurant, where I greeted them and had a glass of wine to settle my nerves. Expectations were high, although I tried to lower them by telling Gorton that a fourth place finish would be an excellent start, while secretly wanting Yaldas Girl to win by three lengths.

She was a lengthy, rakish, athletic grey filly by Unbridled's Song, who had cost $200,000 as a yearling. On the gallops, Yaldas Girl had displayed considerable skill in getting rid of her rider, managing to put one girl in hospital twice. Since then she had become more amenable and, although she wasn't mature mentally, Yaldas Girl had shown enough ability at home to give us confidence that she would perform well.

We all went down to the parade ring, where Yaldas Girl was a bit nervy but looked great. Jamie Spencer was riding and, on the way down, Gorton's filly looked encouragingly relaxed. On Racing UK, Eddie Fremantle awarded her an unsolicited plus mark. So far, all was going well. Not for long.

Things started to go wrong when the stalls handlers invited Yaldas Girl to enter the stalls. When they finally got her in, her tail got trapped. When she came out, she went sideways, didn't look happy, and finished a well-beaten last of ten. Oh, no.

Mercifully, I wasn't watching it with Gorton because, if I had been, I might have stabbed myself in the jugular with the nearest fork and hoped for some sympathy. I'm not sure I'd have got any. A man like Gorton is used to success, not failure. His City friends were ribbing him mercilessly. Gorton smiled at me but it was a smile that seemed to say, 'That's $200,000 down the pan. What's your next trick?'

Spencer is an articulate jockey and he told us to ignore the run which, unfortunately, wasn't possible. The filly had got stage fright, he said, and didn't have a clue what she was doing, which I hoped was true. Then Spencer suggested that we find a little race on Polytrack for her because she doesn't bend her knees and needs either very fast ground or Polytrack. That wasn't what I wanted to hear. Gorton hadn't come into racehorse ownership in order to visit Wolverhampton, and I didn't want to suggest that he did. Even I don't like going there much.

John Best chipped in with his opinion. He also thought we should forget the run because, judged on her work at home, Yaldas Girl was a lot better than that. It eased the pain a bit, but not much.

We returned to the restaurant for more teasing. I think

Dave's mates secretly liked the fact that, for once in his life, golden bollocks had got something wrong; or I had. I'd been making jokes about Teddy Grimthorpe and how easy it was being a racing manager; now I was squirming, wondering what I could do to put things right, apart from offer my resignation. It was a baptism of fire.

While I was wondering, Gorton went home, unhappy. At that moment, the glorious uncertainty of horseracing seemed to have lost some of its charm. The next morning Gorton evidently got a text message reading, 'Great picture of your race in the *Racing Post*. I can't see your horse in it.'

They say that the worse a horse runs, the longer the post mortem, as every conceivable excuse is explored. Ours would have lasted more than an hour if Best and I hadn't had to set off for Kempton's evening meeting, where Mullionmileanhour was making his debut for Kent Bloodstock. John went to Kempton while I went to the Racing UK studio.

I had intended to have several thousand pounds on Mullionmileanhour, who was a straightforward horse, and a fast one. Only two days earlier, Best had been telling us that Mullionmileanhour could be as good as Kingsgate Native. John isn't a punter and, in the car, he told me that I couldn't back the horse now, after Yaldas Girl's poor run. I was inclined to agree.

My confidence was shaken. Maybe there was a bug in the yard, and Jamie Osborne's newcomer, The Dial House, was said to be a Royal Ascot prospect. On Betfair, Mullionmileanhour was over 20-1. Soon, on television, I would be asked about his chances, and whether or not I'd backed him. I had £222 at 23-1. One of the partners in Kent Bloodstock had £300 each-way, which helped send the price tumbling towards Mullionmileanhour's SP of 10-1. I told viewers that, if it weren't for the fact that Yaldas Girl had run so disappointingly, I would really fancy the horse.

From early on, Mullionmileanhour looked the winner. Liam Keniry, who had been impressed by the horse at home, had him perfectly placed, and everything went his way, partly because Mullionmileanhour was quick enough to take advantage of the gaps that opened up for him. He got a dream run, but would have won without one. Mullionmileanhour looked very professional, and won impressively.

It was a great result for Kent Bloodstock, I'd won five grand, and emails of congratulation started to arrive at the studio. Yet every time I was off camera, I put my head in my hands. I knew how well the horse had been working and I trusted Best's judgement that he was a bit special; and you could back him at 20-1 and more. What was I doing? What was the point of having knowledge like that and not using it? After all, that was part of the attraction of being involved in buying and managing horses, that you got to know more about them. I knew I'd just missed a great opportunity.

Yaldas Girl's run had been doubly damaging. If she had run better, or her race had been after Mullionmileanhour's, I would have had a £3,000 or £4,000 bet. I probably wouldn't have got 20-1 for all of it, but I'd have won upwards of £50,000. You shouldn't complain when you win £5,000, but I did.

*

Mullionmileanhour's success removed the fear that there might be something wrong with the stable's horses, and Flashmans Papers' debut at Windsor a few days later, on April 21, went some way towards compensating Dave Gorton for the Yaldas Girl debacle.

Flashmans Papers is a totally different physical specimen, a stocky, chunky, powerful sprinter. I walked the course beforehand and gave Liam Keniry his instructions, which he carried out to the letter. Flashmans Papers travelled well through the race and finished third, beaten a length and a half. He just ran out of puff but would probably have finished second if the winner, Miss Chamanda, hadn't crossed him.

Gorton wasn't there, making me think, here we go, he's lost interest already, but he did back Flashmans Papers each-way, at 9-1, so it wasn't a bad result. I don't think Flashmans Papers is as good as Mullionmileanhour but he's not far behind and good enough, hopefully, to run at Royal Ascot. That's what I want to achieve for Gorton.

We hoped to win a maiden race with him before Ascot and, a fortnight later, ran Flashmans Papers on Kempton's Polytrack. When I saw the draw, one of ten, in a race where the draw mattered, I swore. As it happened, it cost our horse ground but it didn't cost him the race. There was a brief moment when I thought Flashmans Papers might win; in the end he was just run out of second place, looking as if he might be a short runner.

The winner, Shampagne, won his next race and then ran in the Coventry Stakes at Royal Ascot but it was still disappointing, and Gorton was certainly disappointed. He is used to making successful investments and I have to try to acclimatise him to the realities of racing, where success, particularly at the higher levels, is far from inevitable or routine. Experience has made me have expectations that are deliberately on the low side so that, when things do go right, you really appreciate it, and it is exciting. I have to lower Gorton's expectations without letting him down so heavily that I lose him as a client. On a smaller scale than Lord Grimthorpe, I am feeling the pressure of being a racing manager.

What do we do now? I've been told that, if you are hoping to sell a two-year-old to the USA, it must win in its first three outings. Should we just try to find a weak maiden race for Flashmans Papers, or press on to Royal Ascot?

Flashmans Papers and Mullionmileanhour were entered for both the Listed Windsor Castle Stakes on the opening day of Ascot and for the Group 2 Norfolk Stakes two days later. Apart from the Molecomb Stakes at Goodwood in July, the Flying Childers at Doncaster in September, and the Cornwallis Stakes at Ascot in October, the Norfolk is the only Group race over five furlongs open to two-year-old colts and geldings, unless they take on older sprinters in the Nunthorpe at York in August, as Kingsgate Native did so triumphantly last year. If we wanted to go for Group races, there wasn't a lot of choice, particularly with Flashmans Papers, who looked as if he probably wouldn't stay beyond five furlongs.

Gorton still had other potential Ascot horses, in the shape of Square Eddie and Elegant Cad. We ran Square Eddie in a conditions race at Windsor on May 19. On the face of it, it wasn't a Royal Ascot performance. Starting at 22-1, Square Eddie finished third of four. In reality, it was a really good first effort, good enough to justify going for the Coventry Stakes.

I was at Musselburgh that day, working for Racing UK, and watched the race from a local betting shop. On Betfair, Square Eddie was trading at 90-1, so I had to back him. I knew he had a better chance than that.

There were only four runners, but they were good ones. White Shift had beaten The Dial House in a maiden race at Great Leighs and then finished third in a reasonable conditions race at Chester. Sayif, making his debut and odds-on, cost 200,000 guineas and was subsequently narrowly beaten in the Group 2 July Stakes at Newmarket before finishing third in the Group 2 Vintage Stakes at Goodwood. White Shift beat Sayif by a short head, with Square Eddie only a length further back, showing both speed and purpose. Square Eddie was cut off when making his move between horses. Liam Keniry had to pull him wide, after which Square

Eddie ran on again, showing a positive attitude. If the three horses met again, there was a good chance that he would be the winner. Behind him, fourth and last, was Fault, who had won a maiden race at Windsor on his only previous start.

On Derby day, June 7, it was Elegant Cad's turn, in a conditions race at Musselburgh. I felt I should be there to represent Gorton, so I missed being at Epsom for the first time for many years. Elegant Cad had been working very well with Meydan Dubai, a three-year-old who, the previous day, had finished midfield in a handicap at Epsom off a rating of 86. Judged on his home work, Elegant Cad could be a serious racehorse.

Although I'd told several people that we thought he was good, I was still amazed to see that he was trading at 10-1 on Betfair rather than twice those odds. I backed him, but not heavily. There were only six runners but two of them had won their previous races. One of them, Spin Cycle, would later be narrowly beaten in the Norfolk Stakes.

In the parade ring, I told Liam Keniry to give Elegant Cad a good introduction, and not knock the horse about, but that we had backed him. He ran well, dwelling slightly in the stalls but then travelling well behind the leaders before getting left behind slightly when they quickened up, then running on strongly towards the finish. Elegant Cad finished fourth, only two lengths behind Spin Cycle. Liam said that he was on the best horse in the race and only got beaten because of the firm ground and Elegant Cad's greenness.

It was yet another very promising debut, and another Royal Ascot runner beckoned for Gorton, probably in the Norfolk Stakes. We would soon find out whether or not any of them could win there for him.

*

NOTTINGHAM
APRIL 23

I am living on a knife edge. It's stressful. Essentially what I am doing is using my winnings from fixed-odds betting, which is going reasonably well, to fund my pool betting, which isn't going well, and has cost us more than £50,000 so far this year. We've had several near-misses on the Jackpot and I've spent the last few days chasing it as the pool has built up.

Yesterday I went to Southwell, which I've rarely visited since the days when I used to bet regularly at their all-weather meetings. It hasn't changed much. It was a lovely sunny day but it still seemed bleak there.

The first race was the most difficult and I was hoping to glean something useful from a paddock inspection. If I was going to put £3,000 or £4,000 into the Jackpot, I thought it was worth having a look at the horses first. I studied them diligently without it prompting me to change my tissue, although I thought Discanti, an outsider trained by Tim Easterby, looked particularly well, so I included him in our perm.

Discanti ran well to be fourth, and subsequently won two races, but my paddock inspection didn't prevent us from being knocked out in the first leg. The race was won by Legendary Guest, at 16-1. On his previous outing, admittedly under different conditions, he had finished last of 12, beaten over 40 lengths. It was a nice 39th birthday present for trainer David Barker and the only thing that cheered me up a bit was that he seemed to have a bigger, redder face than me. I don't know if he'd had a big bet but the result pissed me off anyway.

So it was on to Nottingham, where the pool swelled to over £1.6 million. The first race was a 14-furlong handicap, a trial race for the Chester Cup. The favourite was Puy D'Arnac with Double Banded second in the market, 9-2 in my tissue. When Double Banded came into the paddock he looked like a greyhound who had just stepped out of a Turkish bath. I rang Mark and told him not to include him in any more lines than the ones we'd already submitted. I thought, if this horse wins after sweating like that, I'll give the game up; he cannot win, he's gone from 9-2 to 50-1 with me. I wasn't the only one thinking that because Double Banded drifted from 9-2 to 8-1, then won comfortably. I quivered in disbelief. I wasn't going to give the game up but, in future, I was going to settle for just watching the girls leading the horses round. In the Jackpot, we were now hanging on by a thread.

Paddock observers were adamant that Cabinet, 6-4 favourite for the second race but making his seasonal debut, would definitely need the run. Cabinet would be in almost everyone's Jackpot, including ours, but we had got Eradicate, the third favourite, in almost as many lines. Thanks to a terrific ride by Ryan Moore, Cabinet got up to beat Eradicate by a neck. Pity.

We had put £11,000 into the Jackpot. For it to pay a worthwhile sum, there had to be an upset. Curtain Call, Luca Cumani's Derby candidate, seemed certain to win the three-horse conditions race, at odds-on, and duly did. There was another hot favourite in the fourth race, a sprint handicap in which Chief Editor was 5-4. Could he be beaten? He was a solid favourite but was surrounded by useful early pace horses, and Jamie Spencer would be holding him up. We've all seen them, and we've all backed them, the hold-up rides that Spencer messes up.

Just in case, I backed Canadian Danehill, who was drawn against the rail and was 28-1 on Betfair, and also backed a couple of others. I hoped Spencer wouldn't find a way through and, briefly, it looked as if he might not. He did, to win by three-quarters of a length. Another pity, because Canadian Danehill, second at an SP of 22-1, would have taken almost everyone else out of the Jackpot.

Race five, and another hot favourite. Wasan, who cost 525,000 guineas as a yearling, had been given a handicap rating of 74 after winning a maiden race at Lingfield on his only previous appearance. He wasn't bred to be a 74-rated handicapper and he wasn't likely to remain one. It's unreasonable to expect the official handicapper to make a judgement and allot a rating on the basis of a single run, even a winning one. Every horse should have to run at least twice before being given a rating, and there should be races for the winners of one race, to provide a more accurate view of what such horses are capable of.

Wasan won by six lengths, at 5-4, and was promptly put up to 88. After winning off that mark, he went up again, to 95.

So far, the winners consisted of a joint-second favourite and four short-priced favourites. An awful lot of people were getting ready to join a long payout queue for the Jackpot. All that stood between them and a small dividend was a 14-runner maiden race, in which Ryan Moore was riding the favourite, Ascot Lime, for Sir Michael Stoute. We had five horses running for us but only two of them would return more than we had staked. Mercifully, Tarkheena Prince, the 7-1 winner, was one of the two. If Hawk Island, a neck behind, had won, we would have lost the lot. The Jackpot paid £4,714 and we ended up with a profit of about £3,000. It cost a lot of nervous energy.

*

At the moment, I don't feel in control as much as I want to. There's not enough consistency in my betting performance. The frustrations of near-misses in the Jackpot and Scoop6 don't help.

On April 28, a Monday, I went to Towcester, the scene of my first day as a full-time professional punter, back in 1993. I am wondering whether I should concentrate on jumps meetings for my bread and butter and just go to the better meetings on the Flat, especially as my involvement at John Best's yard, as well as my telephone tipping service and television work with Racing UK, make it more difficult to keep on top of all the form.

I stand by what I said about tipping lines in *A Bloody Good Winner*, that all tipping services are doomed in the long run because the betting market adjusts to accommodate a successful line. An unsuccessful one fails of its own accord, while a successful one eventually depresses the prices available on its selections, making it difficult to show a profit, and the tipping service's customers look elsewhere.

That isn't a criticism of tipping lines, some of which certainly deserved to be maligned in the past but are now generally well-intentioned attempts by competent pundits to give people sound advice. It wasn't always like that. I remember one telephone tipster who used to tell jokes and talk about the blackbirds pulling up worms from his lawn, and generally string the phone call out for as long as possible, at premium rates, until finally tipping a 6-4 favourite. Punters are more knowledgeable now and won't stand for that sort of thing. Nowadays, if you don't provide a proper service, you soon won't have one.

People who think that phoning a tipping line is going to make a material difference to their life are mistaken but I do think it can help improve people's betting. I like to think that punters ring my line because they are interested in hearing my opinion, and hopefully respect my judgement. To the extent that my knowledge and judgement are better than theirs, my contribution should at least help to reduce their losses.

My approach to betting is price-sensitive, and my approach to tipping is the same. I talk about the card for the race meeting I am attending, starting with my thoughts on the first race and ending with my analysis of the last race. If there isn't going to be a nominated bet I say so at the start of the message but then still talk people through the card, for those who still want to listen. There is, of course, the usual problem that if I tell people to take, say, 8-1 with Betfred, and every caller acts on my advice and rings Betfred, the 8-1 will have disappeared. After a shaky start, the line has been going pretty well.

I can fit my telephone service into my day's routine easily enough but trying to pursue a normal day's betting when I am appearing on Racing UK isn't so easy. That is one of the reasons why, to start with, I didn't really enjoy television work. On its own, the pay wasn't enough to support my lifestyle so I would try to carry on betting at the same time. Now, I've worked out how to combine the two more successfully.

I've become a regular member of Racing UK's team and generally appear about once a week, usually at the smaller meetings. That suits me because, at the big ones, I want to concentrate on what I think I do best, which is betting. When I am on Racing UK, I tend not to bet much, particularly since a lot of the time we are looking at awful horses in awful races. If it is an evening meeting, I usually arrive at the studio at midday, do my betting from there in the afternoon, then wind down for the evening coverage.

I like working with Nick Luck and Stewart Machin and think Angus McNae is competent too, although he lacks self-confidence, maybe because it seems to have been decreed that he gets the Alan Partridge slots, equivalent to the early morning show on Radio Norwich. Machin is rock-solid and has a good sense of humour while Luck exudes confidence and has a great depth of knowledge. Some of the words he uses baffle me and how he manages to get them into sentences involving horseracing is beyond me. He certainly went to a different school to the one I went to and talks about French painters as if every kid brought up on a council estate in Halifax is used to studying the works of Degas. I call him Lord Snooty but, although Nick's got a posh accent, he's not arrogant and we get on very well. He's very funny.

I like being in the studio, where you can get a dialogue going with viewers, and I think all the evening meetings should probably be covered from there, rather than from the track. Last winter I went to Kempton for Racing UK a few times and thought it was pointless having an outside broadcast unit. It was freezing, the horses were wearing big rugs in the parade ring and you couldn't learn anything from seeing them.

I don't think it will be long before Kempton isn't covered at all, because it will be occupied by a supermarket. I hope

I am wrong but, unless they introduce a direct train service from Waterloo to Kempton, they are just not going to capture London's evening market. In practice, Kempton provides televised entertainment for betting shops, pubs and clubs and, given that reality, I can't see the commercial justification for having all that land tied up in a racecourse.

I have a similar opinion about Great Leighs. It's a shame but horseracing at a venue like Great Leighs just won't be able to pull in a big crowd, even if they follow Towcester's example, and let everyone in free.

The first race at Towcester that day, April 28, I'd priced Learning The Blues up at 7-4 on. On Betfair, it was 11-10 on. Before I left home, I managed to get just short of £1,000 on at that price. Then I caught a train from Euston to Milton Keynes, got a taxi to the racecourse, set up my laptop in the press room, and discovered that there were three non-runners and that Learning The Blues was now 5-2 on. I didn't feel good about it. In the race, all went well for a while but not for long. Learning The Blues suddenly downed tools and refused to co-operate.

I then backed another David Pipe-trained horse, Reidwil, who was second favourite in a claiming hurdle. He didn't run much better than Learning The Blues.

The day was saved when Lucky Luk won a handicap chase by a short head, at 11-2, but it didn't send me on my way full of confidence, which was in short supply.

*

If you are travelling anywhere by train with Eddie Fremantle, you don't need to consult a timetable. Part of Eddie's brain is reserved for train timetables and if he ever appears on Mastermind, that will be his specialist subject.

It's not just the times of the trains, it's the fares, too. If you are going to Southwell (hard to imagine you'd want to, admittedly), you can't get a ticket in advance from King's Cross station to Rolleston, which is the nearest station to the racecourse, but you can from St Pancras station, even though the train goes from King's Cross. If you get your ticket at St Pancras, then catch a train for Newark from King's Cross, it saves £12. I may have got that wrong, but Eddie won't have. Unfortunately, trying to exploit the curiosities of the fare system seems to have become an obsession with him.

On April 29, the day after Towcester, Eddie and I caught a train to Bath. Eddie had worked out a way of travelling first class for part of the journey for less than if we'd got a standard class ticket the whole way. The downside was that, just as we were getting comfortable, we had to get off at Didcot and buy a standard class ticket for the rest of the journey. What we saved on fares we spent on coffee and cakes in the station buffet while waiting 20 minutes for the next train. Is it worth it?

Usually, I like travelling to racecourses by train. It's fun, and I think courses should make more of the fact that racegoers can get there by public transport, and have a good time on the way.

Not that Eddie and I did, particularly, because it was pouring with rain. Lansdown Hill was like base camp at Mount Everest, but colder. We didn't mind too much for ourselves but we were worried about Dark Missile. Eddie and I agreed that, on form, although an extra furlong would help, she was the only possible winner of the five-furlong Listed Lansdown Fillies' Stakes. Both of us had already backed her, at just under even money. The only danger was the ground, which was officially good.

That was until after the second race, when it became officially good to soft, until after the third race, when it officially graduated to soft. Dark Missile was running in the sixth race. Should we lay Dark Missile, and accept a loss? Instead, we kept telling each other that the race times weren't signalling soft going; they were signalling good to soft. Unfortunately, when the time came, Dark Missile took more time than Morinqua, the winner. The water at Bath may have done wonders for people's arthritis over the centuries but it certainly didn't do me any good.

Just as Lucky Luk had saved the previous day, at Towcester, the day at Bath was saved, for Eddie as well as me, by Pennyspider's win, at over 30-1 on Betfair, in the last race. The fact that our taxi didn't turn up and we were stranded at base camp Everest was more bearable after that, but there still seemed no rhythm to my betting.

Nor on the next, miserably wet and cold, day at Ascot where, along with a room full of other people, we won the

Jackpot. There was a pool of £82,128 and 42 winning tickets, each paying £1,388. We had five winning tickets but our net profit was less than £1,000. It's not the first time we've won the Jackpot this year but, each time we've won it, so has everybody else. To win the sort of amounts we are trying to win, you must have a winner that knocks most people out. We haven't had that kind of winner yet. A couple of times, on the Scoop6 as well as the Jackpot, we've narrowly missed a big payout, but they don't pay out on near-misses.

There would have been far fewer winning tickets if the hot favourite, Bankable, hadn't won the final race. Backing an 11-8 favourite in a 20-runner handicap isn't my thing but backing other horses each-way in a race like that is. I wanted to take the early price of 15-2 against The Snatcher, who started at 9-2. Unfortunately, between me backing him and him starting, five horses were pulled out, meaning that The Snatcher had to finish third rather than fourth for me to win on the place part of my each-way bet. As it happened, it didn't matter, because he finished fifth.

Bankable duly won en route to his target, which was clearly the Royal Hunt Cup at Royal Ascot. I have nothing but praise for Luca Cumani, who is one of the best trainers there is at identifying a suitable target for a horse, and getting it there with a good chance of winning. Bankable has now won twice over the same course and distance as the Hunt Cup, in style, and is clearly better than the rating of 94 that he subsequently took to a Listed race at Goodwood.

He romped home in that and was put up to 113 but, at Royal Ascot, he will be able to run off his old rating of 94, plus a 5lb penalty. It is another cleverly devised plan on Cumani's part.

*

NEWMARKET
MAY 3

Two Thousand Guineas day isn't a massively enjoyable race day any more, even though I am in the privileged position of being able to escape to the press room, which is slightly less scary than elsewhere.

The problem for racecourses is that there aren't enough people with sufficient interest in horseracing to commercially justify the huge areas the courses occupy. As a result, they have to offer other attractions, which in Newmarket's case means drink and music.

At the Friday night meetings on the July course the racing is a sideshow to the concerts and that works pretty well because everyone who goes is expecting there to be music. It doesn't work so well on 2,000 Guineas day, when 40 per cent of the crowd are serious racegoers who want to see the horses and have a bet, while the other 60 per cent, many of them in coach parties, want to get seriously trolleyed, and invariably succeed.

If you want to go from the paddock to the betting ring, passing through the grandstand, you risk getting into a fight because every nudge annoys someone, either the person trying to get through or the one legitimately standing drinking. I didn't see any real trouble but if someone nudged the wrong person, there might well be. The spread for stabbings is probably 1.5-3 and, for deaths, 0-1 but, in the long term, I would want to be a buyer. That's the way things are heading at the Rowley Mile course.

As a racetrack, I've done well there. A lot of punters don't like the big fields you tend to get but I prefer them, as long as the runners don't split into three groups, and run three separate races. When that happens, it probably means that the track has been watered and the jockeys have different views about where the best ground is. In the 2,000 Guineas, the entire field tacked across to the stands side and those drawn wide were seriously disadvantaged. Johnny Murtagh, who is probably the best jockey in the world, had the bottle to sit and wait in the right lane on Henrythenavigator, and managed to get through, whereas Jimmy Fortune had to take the wide road on Raven's Pass.

I had to leave early, having had a big each-way bet on Silver Suitor at 11-2 in the final race, and a covering bet of £555 at 8.5-1 on Ajaan. I listened to the commentary while sitting in the back of a mate's car. Evidently it was like banger racing in the final furlong, after which Ajaan passed the post a head in front of Camps Bay, with Silver Suitor finishing third after suffering interference. People weren't just betting on whether or not Ajaan would keep the race but on whether the first two would both be thrown out.

Graham Cunningham, who also appears on Racing UK, and was at Newmarket, is the best judge of stewards' enquiries and the rule book that I know, so I rang him in the press room. I asked him if he thought Ajaan would keep the race. 'He's got to go, got to go,' said Graham.

'Are you sure?'

'Dave,' he said, 'if they do it by the rules, he's got to go.' Then, as he was looking at the replay, he said. 'Oooh, I don't know . . . I think it'll definitely go.'

On Betfair, Camps Bay was 5-2 on to get the race. I put £2,222 on it. A few seconds later it was evens.

Eventually, the stewards announced that the placings remained unaltered. I had managed to convert an 8.5-1 winner into a 4.5-1 winner, which is the sort of thing you do when you are out of form and lack confidence. I hadn't even seen the race and I'd put over £2,000 on a 5-2 on shot – and nowadays the stewards never throw them out.

Later, when I saw a replay myself, I think the stewards did the right thing. It was an impossible decision to have to make. Whatever they did, they'd be berated. While some punters were berating the stewards, this punter was berating himself.

CHAPTER SIX

CHESTER DAYS . . . AND NIGHTS

CHESTER
MAY 7 – 9

Chester is all about having fun, and making money. If someone wants to offer me 6-4 on against me winning over the three days, I'll take it, because Chester is one of those tracks where I usually win, and I'll be gutted if I don't.

A lot of punters don't like Chester because too many horses have bad luck in-running but I'm prepared for that, and when it happens at my expense it doesn't knock me out of my stride too much. I feel I can get a handle on races at Chester, identifying the ones where the draw will have a big impact and the ones where it won't, because of where the pace is likely to be, and so on. In some of the races over seven and a half furlongs and ten and a half furlongs people tend to exaggerate the effect of the draw, and you can get big prices about horses drawn eight, nine or ten. I'll be looking for that, and at other great sights, particularly on Chester Cup day and Ladies day. Sad to say, I expect I'll be leering at 19-year-old girls.

As usual, I'm staying at the Crowne Plaza Hotel, formerly the Moat House. Nothing stays the same. I used to book five twin rooms for myself and my mates but now we're down to three rooms. Some of my friends' wives have probably cottoned on to the goings-on, so that avenue of pleasure has been denied them. It might be me getting older but the town centre is scarier than it used to be, with more scallywags around and, if you end up in the wrong place late at night, it can be unnerving. It will still be fun.

The plan is to get Wednesday's card done on Tuesday, go back to the hotel after a winning opening day on Wednesday, get most of Thursday's card done by about 6.30pm, then go out with the gang and have a good night on the town. On Thursday morning I'll go for a swim and, after racing, have a quieter evening. I just can't do two proper nights of revelry in a row anymore. On Friday I'm on Racing UK. I don't know if that's what will materialise, but that's the plan.

*

THE FIRST DAY

Getting to Chester is always a pain in the arse, so we usually go up the day before. Graham Godmon, a retired pub landlord, and I arrived at Euston to catch the 12.17pm train and discovered that there weren't any trains, because of a problem with the overhead power lines. It was rumoured that a gang from Eastern Europe had rolled up miles of cable which was now on its way to Albania, where the copper would be extracted.

We couldn't get the 12.17pm from Euston but were told that we could get the 1.20pm from Marylebone which, three changes later, would get us to Chester at 5.26pm. The only way to stop Graham from whining and moaning was to ply him with drink. By the time we were on the leg from Birmingham to Crewe, Virgin Trains were so fed up with us that we were upgraded to first class and given miniature bottles of whisky to keep us happy, if not quiet.

Eventually we arrived at the Crowne Plaza, dumped our

bags and presented ourselves in Chester, which was already bracing itself for Chester Cup day. The net result was that I woke up on Wednesday morning feeling awful and not in the frame of mind I had intended. It didn't matter too much because there was nothing I hugely fancied.

In the first race, the Lily Agnes Stakes, I thought She's A Shaw Thing would probably win but she was a sure thing's price, 5-4 on, which didn't appeal, especially as her two wins had been on softer ground. I ended up buying the *Racing Post* favourites with Sporting Index, at 63. It's 25 points for each winner, 10 points for finishing second and 5 for third. She's A Shaw Thing missed the break and finished fourth. Not a great start.

Sugar Mint was the morning favourite for the Cheshire Oaks but there was a gamble on Sail who, in her previous outing, had been beaten by a horse rated only 71. Sugar Mint drifted out to 5-2 while Sail ended up the 9-4 favourite.

If you wanted to design a horse not built for coping with Chester's tight turns, Sugar Mint would be it. She was enormous. On the other hand, so was Sail. They were both like dray horses, but faster. In the race, Michael Hills made the first move on Sugar Mint but Johnny Murtagh, on Sail, had her covered and won by half a length. As I'd chosen to do the favourite in the *Racing Post*'s betting forecast rather than the SP favourite, the result was worth 10 points instead of 25. Still, it wasn't a disaster.

Before the Chester Cup, Double Banded again looked

like a greyhound, as he had before winning at Nottingham two weeks earlier. I couldn't fancy him, especially at 9-2. Instead, I fancied the 7-2 favourite, Highland Legacy. Jamie Spencer couldn't get him round the bends and he finished fifth, probably because I'd backed him each-way.

It didn't get better, for me or Spencer. Both of us were on King Orchisios in the sprint handicap. I think the horse may have been injured as he came out of the stalls. Anyway, Spencer pulled him up and King Orchisios had to be put down.

To round things off, before the final race I noticed that Allied Powers looked particularly well and decided to back him, at 4-1. It wouldn't have saved me from a losing day but it would have reduced the damage. Betfair was down, I couldn't get through on the phone, I was too late to reach the ring, and I didn't get on. You know what happened after that.

There were only six races, which was probably just as well but meant that it was all over by 4.45pm, which is a long way from closing time. I had already joined Graham and Andy 'Two Earrings' Bell on champagne, along with a one-legged lap dancer. She did have two legs but one of them was in plaster. Andy is always surrounded by a group of middle-aged women. It's amazing what a credit card can do to make you attractive.

Eventually, we ended up in the Fiesta Havana, with a hen party of policewomen from Liverpool. There was a lot of taking down particulars and 'let's be havin' you' jokes. They were very good humoured and it was very funny but by seven o'clock people were already legless. The bars in Chester are so dark that you come out thinking it must be midnight and it's half past eight.

In the past, I've had some fantastic nights at Brannigans nightclub, a converted cinema with an enticing sign reading, 'Drinking, dancing and cavorting'. Sadly, Brannigans has had a facelift and the sign has disappeared. When we tried to get in, it was students only. The large men on the door were bored with groups of men in their forties assuring them that they were students, form students. They told us to fuck off.

My night came to an end when the boys decided it was time to visit the lap dancers at the Platinum Lounge. I preferred the one-legged one.

*

THE SECOND DAY

At Chester, if you get up early enough, you can stand on one of the balconies in the town centre and watch a parade of young flesh, albeit not at its finest, as clubbers stagger home. I don't know if men ever reach the stage where they are happy just to watch but they probably reach that stage anyway.

There was no chance of me making an early morning visit to a balcony. It was an enormous struggle getting out of bed, which turned out to be to my advantage. If I'd managed to get up earlier I'd have worked out that Royalist should have been about 9-4 for the Halifax Handicap but was 9-2. By the time I'd got that far, everyone else had reached the same conclusion and Royalist was 9-4, which saved me from backing him.

As I have said before, I am a great fan of the trainer-jockey combination of Michael Jarvis and Philip Robinson and, when their horse is a short price and Robinson makes the running, it usually wins. Royalist was favourite and, drawn one of 12, Robinson did make the running but he made it at a ridiculously fast pace, looking like an apprentice rather than P.Robinson, god of tactics. I watched with incredulity and thought Royalist did well to stay in front for so long before fading to finish eighth. At least it demonstrated the value of getting pissed and getting up late.

Unfortunately, I didn't get up late enough to avoid backing Multidimensional in the Grant Thornton Huxley Stakes, although I did back Rebecca De Winter, the winner of the two-year-old maiden race.

We were back in the Fiesta Havana in the evening but I was drinking Coca-Cola. At least, I thought I was, until I caught Graham and Andy spiking my drink with vodka. After that we went for a Thai meal and, while they paid their respects in the Platinum Lounge, I went to bed. I like to think it was because I am a professional rather than because I am 46.

*

THE THIRD DAY

Friday dawned with my head relatively clear. I was on Racing UK with Lord Snooty, alias Nick Luck. He kicked things off by asking me what the highlight of the meeting had been so far. Suddenly, I couldn't remember the name of a single horse that had run during the previous two days. Eventually, I came up with something, and then things improved. Nick and I play the posh git-working-class hero double act quite well and it's interesting reading the comments on the Betfair forum later, although it's not somewhere to visit if you are looking for compliments.

Wherever we are, Nick never spends any money on a hotel. Chester was no different. While I was paying £150 a night at the Crowne Plaza, he was staying on a farm owned by one of his posh friends. Each day he turned up at the racecourse with a foil-wrapped sandwich that the maid had doubtless supplied after Nick had finished eating kedgeree for breakfast.

Although, as a general rule, I don't bet when I'm on television, Chester's card was too good to resist, and I had a rare parade ring success in the Dee Stakes. Tajaaweed didn't look like a horse who would be particularly suited to Chester but he looked fantastic, and stood out from the others. At 6-1 on Betfair, he was worth a bet. It's not often I say that Richard Hills rode a terrific race but I thought he did on Tajaaweed, who won despite the track, by a short head.

In the next race, the Ormonde Stakes, I thought Aidan

O'Brien's Macarthur, the 9-4 favourite, was in a different league to his opponents. I'd decided that if he looked fit I'd have a decent-sized bet on him. In the paddock he looked like a 9-4 on favourite. I had £555 on Betfair, then another £1,111.

It was one of those races where, all the way round, you wish you'd had more on. Other people were probably thinking the same and doing something about it, backing Macarthur in-running. I was just standing there, mesmerised, thinking, this is going to win. It did, by four lengths.

Perhaps things were going too well because, in the sprint handicap, I backed the favourite, Chartist, then noticed that Hadaf, the second favourite, looked terrific, so backed that, then decided that one of the outsiders was too long a price, and backed that, as well. Somehow I'd managed to back three horses in an eight-runner race, at combined odds of about 9-4 on. None of them won, which gave Lord Snooty the opportunity to have a posh laugh at my expense. He took it.

The meeting closed with yet another demonstration, not that one was needed, of the thinness of the line separating triumph from disaster. My view of the final race was that Cruise Director was a well-handicapped horse and that, although he hadn't won for three years, he had a very good chance of finally winning again. The drying ground might be against him but, at about 20-1 on Betfair, he was good value. I had £111 on him, three times.

In classic Chester fashion, Cruise Director couldn't get out to make his challenge when Ted Durcan wanted to, flew home and was beaten a short head by Maslak, whose previous successes had all been on all-weather tracks. I was seething, which isn't ideal when you are on television, but in a situation like that, when you have just missed out on winning £6,000, it's impossible to hide your feelings. If Cruise Director had won, it would have been a winning meeting. Instead, it was a losing one, which I had been confident it wouldn't be.

Chester's May meeting is still a favourite of mine but it was a sad journey home, in Nick Luck's car. As we went to the car park, I was carrying a huge bag plus another heavy one containing my computer. As I trotted along, with Nick beside me, I was pouring with sweat. Anyone else would have said, 'Can I carry one of those?' but not Lord Snooty. That's what a public school upbringing does to you, I suppose. I felt like a railway porter. To be fair, Nick was giving me a lift.

We spent the journey bigging up everyone on Racing UK and trashing everyone on At The Races. Racing UK, we convinced ourselves, was the future. That was enjoyable but, when I got back to my flat in London, I threw my bags down and lay on the bed thinking about what might have been. I met up with Natalie, my girlfriend, shared a bottle of wine, and told myself to get up early the next day, for the Scoop6.

CHAPTER SEVEN

ANOTHER WALLED CITY ... YORK

It's 5.00am on Saturday May 10 and I'm already in the internet café on Marylebone. I find it easier to concentrate there than at home. The café is open 24 hours a day and every form of human life, plus a few other forms, are found there. Internet access costs £1 for half an hour but that is too much for some customers, who try to persuade the sullen girl at the desk to give them credit. A man says, "I only want to see something for a minute." He's potless, and she isn't going to give him a smile, let alone credit.

At about 5.20am, a newsagent nearby opens. I get the *Racing Post* then go back to the internet café. The sun is just coming up. Downstairs, men are openly watching hard porn. I print off the Timeform card and start pricing up the races. I want to win the Scoop6.

At about seven o'clock, I text Mark Smith: 'Scoop6 impossible. Jackpot?' In the end, we did both, putting £3,500 into the Scoop6 pool, which grew to more than £340,000, and just over £400 into the Jackpot pool at Ascot, which ended up with almost £80,000 in it.

We had the first two winners at Ascot, including Baharah, at 12-1. The third race, the Victoria Cup, was also the first leg of the Scoop6. It was a 22-runner handicap and we had been ruthless, making Al Khaleej a banker in the Jackpot and having three in our Scoop6, including Al Khaleej and Zaahid, the joint-favourites. Zaahid beat Al Khaleej by a neck, which knocked us out of the Jackpot, in which we had the other five winners, as you do with the Jackpot. The two winning tickets each paid over £28,000.

Now it was up to the Scoop6. We arrived at the final leg, the 4pm at Haydock, holding six of the remaining 16 tickets. The race was a 16-runner sprint handicap. We had the first six in the betting. I was exhausted after Chester and there were very few bets I wanted to have that day, so I didn't go racing. I listened to the commentary on my mobile phone while sitting in Regent's Park with Natalie and a friend of hers, sipping Chablis. It was a photo-finish between the 3-1 favourite, Cape Vale, who we had, and Harbour Blues, at 14-1, who we didn't have. When the commentator finally said: 'It's desperately unlucky for favourite backers and those in the Scoop6,' I knew we had lost.

We didn't lose money because we laid our final leg selections on Betfair but, if Cape Vale had won, the dividend, with ten of the 16 tickets on the favourite, would have been about £24,000. A head away from the Scoop6, a neck away from the Jackpot, on the same day. It was difficult to take.

People who aren't into betting on horseracing don't understand what an experience like that feels like, especially when things haven't been going very well. Natalie and her friend just shrugged their shoulders and said, 'That's unlucky.' I said, 'Please don't say anything else. Please don't take the piss.' I was trying to keep calm when what I really wanted to do was run naked into the nearby duck pond and scream.

It felt worse on Monday when it was back to work on a bunch of awful races I wasn't interested in. Most punters aren't interested in them, which is partly why margins are moving against them. If I was a bookmaker, I wouldn't give punters a chance on those races, either. Bookmakers say that a good all-weather race holds its own against a good turf race but what do they mean by good? Good in terms of profit margins?

The revised system for returning SPs has affected margins and I am suspicious about some of the prices returned on favourites in big handicaps. I wonder whether bookmakers are cutting the odds on horses at the front end of the market, not because of the volume of money for those horses but because they can then lay off their liabilities in the real market, which is Betfair. If you can lay a horse to undiscerning punters at, say, 4-1, then bet it back on Betfair at 5.5-1, that is very good business. You certainly don't hear bookmakers complaining about Betfair nearly as much as they once did, and I think that is partly because they have worked out how to use the exchanges to their advantage.

On course, punters have also been hit by revised each-way terms. Colin Webster and Barry Dennis are just about the only racecourse bookmakers who still offer one quarter the odds a place on the first four in handicaps with 16 or more runners. Everyone else has switched to one fifth the odds. It is still one quarter the odds in betting shops but if you want a decent-sized bet you can't easily get on.

The old terms gave punters a mathematical edge and although you can't expect bookmakers to tolerate that, it is part of a process that has seen the game getting harder for punters. We have had the golden age, and I was lucky enough to choose the right time to become a professional gambler, but punters are getting squeezed now, and it is tough.

I am finding it more difficult to win and more difficult to get enthused because there are so many bad races.

The fact is that I am still reeling from Saturday's experience, and don't feel as confident about York's May meeting as I did about Chester's, and I didn't win there. At York, there seems to be more depth to the races; more runners with realistic chances. While I'm complaining, I should add that I think you get freak results at York when the track has been watered. You find out, too late, that some strips of ground are much softer than others.

As you can see, I'm not heading to the Knavesmire with my confidence at a peak.

*

YORK
WEDNESDAY MAY 14

I got the first race completely wrong. Godolphin hadn't had a winner so far this season and nothing would have induced me to back Folk Opera, a four-year-old filly returning from injury after a year off. They've had a winner now. I backed Tastahil, the runner-up.

Eureka! – as Archimedes used to shout in ancient Greek and old school books. I've found the winner of the seven-furlong handicap, and backed it at 20-1. I don't like backing hold-up horses at York, a course which suits horses ridden close to the pace, and Jamie Spencer overdid the waiting tactics on Generous Thought. I backed Fathsta, who Richard Hughes had near the front the whole way, and went for home first. It wasn't a big bet, but at least it was the right result.

Then it was back to the wrong one again in the Group 2 sprint, won by Assertive. I thought Aidan O'Brien might have improved US Ranger as a four-year-old but, as it turned out, US Ranger was drawn on the wrong side. He was drawn 17 in a 17-runner field and was the only horse with a double-figure draw to finish in the first seven. Everything panned out nicely for Assertive but I wouldn't be surprised if he didn't win again this season and, writing several months later, he hasn't.

What I'm really doing today is looking towards tomorrow because, joy of joys, I think I've found one. I've picked up on something that I don't think other people will have picked up on.

In my opinion, as a trainer, John Panvert used to be a laughing stock. He hasn't got many horses and the ones he's got aren't much good, but he has moved from Kent, where he doesn't seem to have had any gallops, to Devon, where he has. There are signs that it has made a difference. In February a nine-year-old called Wun Chai, who hadn't won since 2004 and was rated 87, won a hurdle race at Wincanton at 50-1. On his next run, again at Wincanton, off a rating of 95, he won again by ten lengths, at 14-1, after which his rating shot up to 115.

Another horse, Noddies Way, best known for having been the last horse to finish in the 2006 Derby, at 500-1, finally won a race recently, on his 20th attempt. It was a three-runner race at Lingfield but it showed that he might have improved a bit, and the handicapper only raised Noddies Way one pound, to 61.

Panvert isn't much good at placing his horses but he's managed to put Noddies Way in the right race, which is a pretty uncompetitive 0-80 handicap over two and a quarter miles here at York tomorrow, with Kerrin McEvoy booked to ride. It's the last race of the day. It's going to be a long, nervous wait.

I spent the first part of it in the Waterfront restaurant with Andy 'Two Earrings' Bell, waiting for the lobster.

*

THURSDAY MAY 15

The problem when you want to back a horse at a long price is getting on without the price collapsing. Mark Smith and I waited for the bookmakers' morning prices to come up. Noddies Way was generally 12-1, with a bit of 14-1. We took the view that, since there was no activity on Betfair, we'd wait until half an hour before the race, which was at 4.55pm.

I studied the rest of the card. Nothing attracted me, so I spent my time flicking backwards and forwards between oddschecker.com and betfair.com, keeping an eye out for any action involving Noddies Way. There wasn't any until about 12.30pm. Then, just as I was getting ready to go to the track, the price collapsed. If what I was told later was correct, Panvert had been saying that Noddies Way would win. Colin Webster, the bookmaker, evidently also fancied it.

We were in a frenzy. I'd primed Thailand and Zambia, two of my best putters-on, and now I unleashed them with instructions to try to get 14-1, although I knew that would probably be impossible. Getting large sums on at all each way is very difficult and sometimes a putter-on will proudly report that they've got on, without much regard to the price. I've sometimes asked someone to get on at 7-2 and they've rung back, pleased with themselves for having got on at 11-4. When I seem less than delighted, they'll say, but it's going to win, isn't it? It might win but the idea is to have the odds in your favour, not in the bookmaker's. I have known several bright people who have a thorough understanding of prices in the market they work in, and wouldn't dream of paying 25 per cent above their target price for a product yet don't seem to appreciate that the same principles apply in the betting market.

In the end, we managed to put on about £7,000 to win and rather less for a place, at average odds of just over 10-1. We also bought Noddies Way for £125 at about 9 on a 50-30-20-10 spread betting index. If he won, we'd win close to £100,000.

When that much is at stake, it tends to focus the mind. There was some exciting, high-quality racing, including

Tartan Bearer's victory in the Dante Stakes, but I couldn't help thinking about the 0-80 handicap at the end of the card. All afternoon, I sat in my chair in the press room looking across at the winning post. I just wanted the race to be run.

Eventually, the time came. With Greg Wood, the Guardian's racing correspondent, standing next to me, I watched Noddies Way go down to the start. Greg told me to tear my ticket up, because the horse was going to the start like Lochsong, a famous sprinter. Noddies Way was a bit keen but I knew he would run a decent race. Others clearly agreed; he started the 11-2 second favourite.

Mister Arjay made the running, as I'd expected, and McEvoy had Noddies Way in a perfect position, up with the pace the whole way. Gradually horses moved up to challenge, then their challenges petered out. About two furlongs out, when McEvoy asked Noddies Way for an effort, I thought he might just win but Mighty Moon, who I didn't think would get the trip, was going well. I was praying that Mighty Moon's stamina would run out, leaving Noddies Way to battle it out with Mister Arjay, but Mighty Moon stayed the trip well and, in the end, won comfortably, with Mister Arjay beating Noddies Way, who was totally one-paced, by a neck for second place.

It ended up being one of those races where I felt I had pretty much got it right and, by anyone's standards other than those of the mega-wealthy, it was a cracking earner and a great day's pay. I won about £9,000 but kept thinking about the other £91,000 that would have gone with it had Noddies Way won.

I stopped thinking about it after a spell in the Cock and Bottle on Skeldergate, and stopped thinking about it even more after we went to a champagne reception to mark the opening of a new spa in York. We thought it might involve sitting in a pool drinking champagne with naked ladies but it actually involved being handed leaflets and asked if we'd like a facial. Instead, we opted for Kennedy's Cafe Bar in Little Stonegate, where the normal deterioration took place.

I got into conversation with an exceptionally attractive looking lady, who was a lot of fun. Together, we discovered venues I'd never been to before, namely the Biltmore Bar in Swinegate and the Voodoo Lounge, possibly in some other gate. I know we ended up in a taxi miles outside York at 2.30am. When I finally got back to the Queens Hotel, at 4am, my roommate said, 'How's momsy?' so maybe my vision was slightly impaired.

So was my ability to write 1,000 words for the *Daily Record* on Friday morning and put in a perky appearance on Racing UK in the afternoon. Mark had to hold the fort on the betting front.

*

FRIDAY MAY 16

A non-event until the evening. I'd decided to stay overnight and then go on to Newmarket, where half of the next day's Scoop6 races were being run.

We met up with a couple of women we'd met the previous evening and went to a steakhouse for dinner. To give you an idea of the class of company we were keeping, when the waiter asked one of the women how she'd like her steak done, she replied, 'fanny pink.' It was obviously a regular request because the waiter just jotted it down on his pad and the steak arrived, as ordered.

The thought of Saturday's Scoop6 prompted me to make an early escape with a view to making an early start the next morning. I was in bed by 9pm but at 9.45pm the boys appeared, their intentions for the evening having gone unfulfilled, and tried to persuade me to go out again. When I declined, they tried to drag me out of bed by my feet, but I resisted.

CHAPTER EIGHT

ON THE YO-YO

Several trains and station cafés later, I arrived at Ely with Andy 'Two Earrings' and the two Steves, the young one and the fat one. We got a cab and Fat Steve told us a story about an alley next to De Niro's nightclub in Newmarket.

One night, Steve was in the queue for the toilet at De Niro's when he decided he couldn't wait any longer, so he went outside and used the nearby alley. Unfortunately, he wasn't alone. A policeman apprehended him, provoking Steve into using intemperate language, prompting the police officer to handcuff him and bundle him into the back of a police van. Raising the stakes, Steve announced that he had a pocket full of anthrax and was going to kill everyone. Coming, as it did, shortly after the terrorist attack on the World Trade Centre, Steve's announcement was not well received. The police van was driven to Bury St Edmunds police station, where Steve was stripped.

As his pockets were emptied, and an impressive wad of banknotes placed on the counter, Steve said, 'That's more than you lot earn in three months.' Fairly rapidly, he was consigned to a cell. Later, a police sergeant acknowledged that Steve was an unlikely candidate for the post of al-Qaeda terrorist but pointed out, 'you can't be too sure.' Steve was fined for public indecency.

For such a harmless person, Steve has had more than his fair share of brushes with the law. He owns a small block of flats. One night, unable to get home and the worse for drink, he remembered that one of the flats was unoccupied. He'd sleep there. At 2.30am, he went into the flat and passed out on the settee, which alarmed the couple living there, who called the police. Steve had opened the wrong door.

*

Mark and I had a serious go at the Scoop6, putting more than £10,000 into a pool that reached almost £650,000. Looking at the races, I thought it would definitely be won but that it would be very difficult to win. It proved too difficult for us; we went out in the fourth leg, when Strategic Mission went in, at Newbury, at 16-1. That was our Noddies Way profit gone.

Not, thankfully, for long. The next day, Sunday May 18, there was over £180,000 in the Jackpot at Ripon. The first race, a seller, was won by Kim Tinkler on Kneesy Earsy Nosey, who was backed into 8-1. I was one of the small band of punters still alive afterwards, and was probably also one of few who knew the origin of the horse's name. It comes from a scene in a 1933 film called Fra Diavolo, or The Devil's Brother, starring Stan Laurel and Oliver Hardy. While sitting in an inn, Stan plays a game called Kneesy Earsy Nosey, in which you slap both knees, then cross your arms and grab an ear with one hand and your nose with the other, then slap your knees again, cross your arms and grab the other ear and the same nose. Like everything else, there's a clip of it on youtube.com. Stan's very good at the game while Olly isn't.

The Ripon success was timely because, earlier in May, the Los Angeles chapter of the International Laurel and Hardy

Society held its first kneesy-earsy-nosey competition. It was won by Isabela Melendez. I don't suppose she was at Ripon, which was a pity because, if she had been, I'm sure she'd have backed the winner.

We had put less than £800 into the Jackpot because there was a real danger that the favourites would do well and the dividend be small. In the event, although the longest-priced winner after Kneesy Earsy Nosey was 13-2, there were only 5.5 winning tickets, each paying £23,777. We had 50p's worth.

It was like a yo-yo, winning £10,000 one day, losing it the next, winning it again the day after. It wasn't really what my betting business plan envisaged. It might be a good thing that I was about to spend a few days in Cornwall with Lotte, my wife, from whom I am separated, and our children.

I must try to avoid a row with Lotte and buying fish and chips from Rick Stein's fish and chip shop, where something called Gurnard and chips costs £10.95 to take away. Still, better we all sit on the harbour wall eating that than go to Stein's Seafood Restaurant, also in Padstow, where Monkfish Vindaloo costs £28.50.

Cornwall's a long way from Redcar but, unfortunately, not far enough to put me off getting involved in the Jackpot there on Bank Holiday Monday, May 26.

When I was growing up, you couldn't carry The Sporting Life on bank holidays unless you'd been weightlifting at the gym because it was thick with race meetings. On the same

Bank Holiday Monday 20 years ago, there were 14 meetings, compared with today's five. Racecourses don't want to race, even though it's a day when the public can come, because they can't attract corporate clients, who are the ones they are most interested in. The nearest meeting to London was Leicester, which is a pretty appalling state of affairs for a national sport. It meant that several of the worst courses in the country were given the chance to steal the show, such as it was.

As the Jackpot built up, I was half-hoping it would be won, partly because if I got involved, I'd be in trouble with Lotte for walking round with a mobile phone pressed to my ear when I should be devoting myself to the kids, and partly because I never win at Redcar. When you have to drive through a graveyard to get into the racecourse, as you do at Redcar, it's a warning worth heeding. The only consolation is that you don't know you've lost until the horses actually pass the post because they come straight at you and until the closing stages you can't tell whether the one you've backed is fourth or tenth.

I didn't need to be on the phone for long because we were knocked out by the first winner, Rowayton, an unraced two-year-old trained by James Bethell. If that hadn't knocked us out, the winner of the next race would have done. It was a selling race featuring 20 horses. Half the runners had once been able to pick their hooves up but no longer could while the other half had never been able to. The winner was Lewis

Lloyd, at 33-1. Lewis Lloyd hadn't won since 2006 and on his latest run had been pulled up in a selling hurdle at Kelso.

Needless to say, no-one won the Jackpot, which moved on to Chepstow. Since my record there isn't much better than at Redcar, I should have taken us all to the Seafood Restaurant and ordered the most expensive meals available, to save money. I think it was greed that made me carry on chasing the Jackpot but I wasn't greedy enough to put Penny's Gift, the favourite in the first race, into our perm. The Jackpot wasn't won at Chepstow and then wasn't won at Yarmouth, either, by which time there was almost £460,000 in the pool, including the £12,000 Mark and I had 'invested'. The Jackpot was back at Yarmouth again on Thursday, May 29, when the pool topped £1 million; 3.5 winning tickets each paid over £200,000. We weren't one of the 3.5, having overlooked Valatrix in the first. It would have been nice to have got past the first.

That evening, at Sandown, I backed Punjabi at 11-8 on. He won, at 11-10 on. Then I backed Royal And Regal, at evens. He lost. One way and another, it was a very bad week.

*

EPSOM
JUNE 6 AND 7

I like both days of Epsom's Oaks and Derby meeting, not just because of the Classics but because there are four handicaps for four-year-olds and above, races in which I know the horses well.

I was pleased to arrive, in a taxi from Epsom station, but I arrived lacking confidence. I was hoping to restore it. There were two Godolphin horses in the first race on the Friday, the Diomed Stakes, with Alexandros the 100-30 favourite and Young Pretender 7-1. I thought there were holes in both of them, wanted to oppose them and backed three others, including the winner, Blythe Knight. At least, I hoped I'd backed the winner. I'd sent a text to one of my putters-on with my betting instructions but, by the time the race was run, I hadn't received confirmation back. Fortunately, before the second race he texted me to say that his battery was flat but the bets were on, which was a huge relief. I managed to take the wrong price, 9-2 when Blythe Knight's SP was 6-1, but still won over £4,000.

I followed that up by backing Little White Lie at what I thought was an amazing price, 12-1, in the second race, and he won. I was beginning to feel more confident.

The two races I'd already decided I didn't want to play in were the Coronation Cup and the Oaks. The Coronation Cup was a fantastic race and I fancied Getaway but I didn't fancy him at 5-4 even though, in the paddock, he looked terrific while Soldier Of Fortune was sweating like mad. I don't know if that's normal for him but it didn't stop people backing him.

Soldier Of Fortune was one of three Aidan O'Brien runners. Song Of Hiawatha, the pacemaker, shot off in front followed by stablemate Macarthur, who was a genuine contender. Getaway didn't handle the track and rolled towards the far rail, behind Macarthur, making it easy for Johnny Murtagh, challenging on Soldier Of Fortune, to make sure Getaway stayed there. You couldn't say it was a team act but things certainly went their way. Coolmore has so many good horses to play.

Unlike Godolphin this season. They won the subsequent heritage handicap with Emirates Skyline and Frankie Dettori celebrated with a flying dismount but celebrating like that after winning with a five-year-old gelding rated 103 devalues his trademark dismount and isn't what Godolphin are really about, or used to be. Godolphin was about establishing an academy of excellence to promote Dubai. To some extent, in my opinion, that seems to have been lost.

When a race has a lot of horses with Timeform's 'p' next to their names, indicating that they are likely to improve, as I've said before, I don't usually want to play. The Oaks fell into that category. It didn't stop Racing UK's Steve Mellish, a very selective punter, from backing the 33-1 winner, Look Here. Steve told me that, early each year, he and his co-presenter Lydia Hislop went through the Oaks entries and put a line through all the horses who wouldn't stay the mile-and-a-half trip, which was most of them. Being by Hernando out of a Rainbow Quest mare, there were no stamina doubts about Look Here, which qualified her for their shortlist. It was a sound approach, and I may follow their example next year. Unfortunately, Mellish told me ten minutes after the race rather than ten minutes before it.

Seb Sanders' job was made easier by Johnny Murtagh's strange decision to set off at 100mph on Adored. Maybe the O'Brien camp, which accounted for six of the 16 runners, was determined to test the dubious stamina of Lush Lashes, the favourite. They succeeded, but it was suicidal for Adored, and played into Look Here's hands.

She may have been a 33-1 winner that got away but at least I backed Godolphin's second winner of the day, Iguazu Falls, despite the fact that I was standing next to John Best as the horses went down to the start. Best said he thought Iguazu Falls looked lame, which persuaded me to reduce the size of my bet, which was a shame, because Iguazu Falls won by four lengths. It made me wonder how lame the others were.

Derby day opened with the opportunity to back my theory that Sir Michael Stoute's Conduit was likely to win the ten-furlong heritage handicap and that 11-8 wasn't a bad price. Stoute had won the equivalent race with Lord Mayor in 2004 and Stage Gift in 2006 and Conduit looked very much a horse to follow after finishing third on his seasonal debut in a very competitive handicap at Sandown in April. Ryan Moore is riding incredibly well at the moment and, just as I was thinking he had overdone the waiting tactics, he powered down the straight, from last to first, and won by six lengths.

Given his subsequent performances, that wasn't surprising. After the handicapper raised Conduit from 85 to 98, he was runner-up in the Group 2 King Edward VII Stakes at Royal Ascot and then, rated 112, won the Group 3 Gordon Stakes at Goodwood.

When Smokey Storm won the Woodcote Stakes, at 4-1, everything was going swimmingly. I then backed Lady Gloria for the Princess Elizabeth Stakes, at 16-1. She won, at 7-1. Things were going more swimmingly still.

In the five-furlong 'Dash', I backed Holbeck Ghyll, a sprinter best when weaving his way through a big field, off a fast pace. The 'Dash', with 19 runners and pace guaranteed, was ideal for him. When you have races where the horses are good, and you know their characteristics and requirements, it is easier to work out what is likely to happen. In the 'Dash', the runners tend to crowd towards the stands', rail. Holbeck Ghyll was drawn well away from the rail, in stall eight, with Masta Plasta, who was certain to fly down the centre of the track, drawn six. Holbeck Ghyll should get towed along perfectly and William Buick had improved as a jockey since riding in the race last year.

The more I looked at it, the more I liked Holbeck Ghyll's chance. I had £2,000 each-way at 8-1 and Mark had another £550 each-way for us at 15-2. I was in the press room at Musselburgh, where Elegant Cad had just made a promising debut, and it was a brilliant race to watch. As the camera angle changed, I could see Holbeck Ghyll getting nearer and nearer to putting his head in front, and then doing so. It was a great result for us, and it suddenly became very noisy in the Musselburgh press room.

Although I am not keen on betting ante-post in the Classics, and have a poor record when I have, I'd backed two for the Derby – Curtain Call and Tajaaweed. I was right that they would be shorter prices on the day but both ran disappointingly.

I'd probably still have backed them at the prices even if I'd known that New Approach was going to run but I don't know why Jim Bolger, New Approach's trainer, behaved as he did, saying that New Approach definitely wouldn't run, then running him. There were certainly a lot of bets struck on the basis that New Approach was going to be a non-runner.

Ante-post betting on the Classics is a dangerous and unattractive game. If you can get 33-1 about a horse you think will start at 8-1, fine, but it is risky because there are several other options available to potential runners, particularly for those owned by big owners, with teams of horses. It is different, and safer, taking a price on a Monday about a big Saturday jumps handicap, such as the Totesport Trophy Hurdle at Newbury in February, or the Paddy Power Gold Cup Chase at Cheltenham in November, where horses are definitely intended runners. I prefer doing that.

*

Epsom was good for us. We are now over £60,000 up on Betfair and off-course bets for the year but more than £100,000 down on our Tote bets. We have landed several Jackpots but not big ones, which is driving me mad.

The latest frustration was at Nottingham on June 11, when there was £1,178,280 in the pool. When Mark and I are doing the Jackpot, I usually price the horses up and he organises them into perms. I suggested eight lines costing a total of about £3,200. Mark rang to say that he had trimmed two of the lines, which saved £400.

I was on Racing UK and, after Uramazin had won the second race at Nottingham, at 7-1, I got an apologetic text message from Mark. Uramazin was one of the horses he had knocked out. At least I knew the situation from an early stage. Needless to say, if he had left the lines untrimmed, we would have won the Jackpot, and over £45,000. It was a big disappointment and I was more than a little fed up, but it happens.

Being £40,000 down doesn't make good reading and it is a lot of money but, as the Nottingham episode illustrates, it only represents one decent Jackpot win. The situation is worrying and it is a struggle but it would be more worrying if we were losing £40,000 on Betfair, because that would mean that we were getting a lot wrong. We aren't.

What I do know is that I can't make myself rich from fixed-odds betting. I can make a good living and what others would think was a very good living but, after expenses, not make massively life-changing profits. It is a good life but seriously hard work, and I still think we are right to focus on the Jackpot and Scoop6.

I still want to extend my involvement in bloodstock, buying and selling horses and managing them for owners who, together or alone, can afford to buy decent ones.

Since winning a maiden race at Kempton in April, Mullionmileanhour, who cost Kent Bloodstock 26,000 guineas, has been sold for £300,000 to Pattern Racing UK Ltd, in which two of the original group of owners are involved. As a director of Kent Bloodstock, I am eligible for a bonus. Mullionmileanhour is due to run at Royal Ascot in the Windsor Castle Stakes.

So is Flashmans Papers, for Dave Gorton, who will also have Square Eddie running in his colours in the Coventry Stakes and Elegant Cad in the Norfolk Stakes. After his promising debut at Windsor, we received an offer of $400,000 for Square Eddie, twice what we paid for him, to go to the USA. After discussing it with Gorton, we put a price of $600,000 on him. The potential buyer sent an agent over to look at the horse, liked him, but wasn't prepared to pay $600,000. Gorton is a businessman but doesn't need to sell and wants to see his horses run at Royal Ascot, so we stuck to our asking price.

John Best's mandate, for both Gorton and Kent Bloodstock, was to get horses to Royal Ascot, and get the best value for them for their owners. I think he does that very well. Now we are hoping that the horses perform equally well.

CHAPTER NINE

THE JOYS AND DESPAIRS
OF ROYAL ASCOT

ROYAL ASCOT
TUESDAY JUNE 17

R oyal Ascot is an even bigger meeting than usual for me this year because three of Dave Gorton's two-year-olds are running, as well as stablemates Mullionmileanhour and Kingsgate Native, the winner of last year's Nunthorpe Stakes. I think John Best has done well to get three of Gorton's to Ascot, each with decent outside chances. When the owner looks at the racecard and sees how much some of the other horses cost, I think he will agree.

Royal Ascot is a meeting where, on the betting front, I always expect to win because the market is very competitive and the margins therefore narrower. Having said that, the card on the opening day this year doesn't appeal from a betting point of view. It is fantastic racing, but not a day for me. I am hoping it will be a fantastic day for Dave Gorton.

Having said that I wouldn't get involved, it was disappointing that I did, backing Cesare each-way in the opening Queen Anne Stakes. He finished fourth, a neck behind the third, at 15-2. Jamie Spencer did what I think he does too often for a top-class jockey, find trouble on a hold-up horse. I wonder how the owners, Cheveley Park Stud, felt as Cesare was led in. I know how I felt.

It was another race shaped by Aidan O'Brien's runners, with Honoured Guest the pacemaker and stablemate Mount Nelson arguably helping the winner, Haradasun. I can't find a case for banning pacemakers and the jockeys did nothing wrong but racing is not a team game and, although the best tactics won, I'm not sure that the best horse did.

The King's Stand was a terrific race. I wanted Kingsgate Native to win but he hadn't run for eight months and, having shown his worth as a two-year-old, now had to prove himself again as a three-year-old. It was a big ask. Fleeting Spirit was too short at 15-8, as I think a lot of Jeremy Noseda's fancied horses are, and I had £333 at 29-1 on the winner, Equiano, who started at 22-1. I thought he was overpriced. That secured a quiet betting day.

Then it was the Coventry Stakes, and Square Eddie. In the parade ring, he didn't look out of place and, after the pleasantries were over, I took my place in the stand, conscious of Dave Gorton in the restaurant above me. The financial markets have been tough recently, so Gorton didn't have his usual box. Square Eddie was 40-1 and, after racing keenly, finished 11th of 18. I thought he ran creditably, without setting the world alight but I think Gorton had been expecting better. 'He didn't beat many, did he?' he asked.

My focus was on Square Eddie but, betting, I'd opposed the favourite, Orizaba, who had won a maiden race at Newbury by nine lengths. Horses who have won their only race to date by a wide margin often start at a false price next time they run. Orizaba finished fifth, with the race won by Jamie Spencer on Art Connoisseur. Having failed to shine on Cesare, Spencer rode a great race. That's Spencer.

There were 25 runners for the Windsor Castle Stakes, including John Best's trio, Mullionmileanhour, Flashmans

Papers and Kingsgate Storm, the last named owned by John Mayne, the owner of Kingsgate Native. Ascot may be too stiff a track for Flashmans Papers, but he is fast and has improved, while I think Mullionmileanhour has a real chance. Before the race, Best told me that I shouldn't leave Flashmans Papers out of my bets because he had worked well recently with Mullionmileanhour. Mullionmileanhour went off at 16-1, which I thought was a very attractive price; Flashmans Papers was 100-1. I had about £3,500 on Mullionmileanhour and, on Betfair, had £55 at over 160-1 on Flashmans Papers. I still didn't expect Flashmans Papers to win, and told Gorton that we were there to enjoy ourselves. His horse had improved, but wasn't going to win.

During the race, I heard Yalda, Gorton's wife, ask where their horse was. He was plumb last, and was still last inside the two-furlong marker. I felt as if my career as a racing manager was on the line, and possibly about to sink beneath it. Then, like Art Connoisseur in the Coventry Stakes, Flashmans Papers took off. Watching him pass horse after horse, and then take the lead, was brilliant, a fantastic feeling.

I ran to the restaurant to find Dave and Yalda but couldn't see them. We were on our mobile phones to each other, trying to make contact. When we finally did, Gorton was thrilled to bits. His first winner as an owner, and it was a Royal Ascot winner! What a place to start.

In the winner's enclosure, jockey Steve Drowne said, 'He's got some boot. I thought I'd better give him a tap with the whip and he passed a few, so I gave him another one, and he flew.' The atmosphere was terrific, and so many people came up and congratulated us.

Afterwards, we had a post-race celebration in the car park, where I met a very interesting man who had been Hugh Hefner's business partner. Unfortunately, we talked more about racehorses than Playboy centrefolds. Trainer David Evans was there, accepting drinks, as was trainer David Elsworth, who eventually went off in a huff. We left as it was getting dark and ended up in a Thai restaurant. It was great fun.

One way and another, it was a seriously good day. I won over £15,000 from betting, and Flashmans Papers' win was priceless. I just hope it doesn't make Gorton believe that it is easy.

*

WEDNESDAY JUNE 18

I think Aqlaam has been seriously underrated and overpriced for the Jersey Stakes. I was very impressed by his winning performance in a maiden race at Newbury last month and it wouldn't surprise me if he ends up as a Group 1 horse. After last night's celebrations, I wasn't up early enough to get hold of the 11-1 but, throughout the race, I was happy with my £1,000 at 7-1 plus £333 on Betfair at slightly better odds. He won comfortably. Evidently trainer William Haggas had wanted to run Aqlaam in tomorrow's Britannia Stakes handicap, off his rating of 93. If that had happened, I think several people would have become millionaires, possibly including me.

In the next race, the Windsor Forest Stakes, I had a small bet on the winner, Sabana Perdida, second favourite to Heaven Sent, because she'd won a Group 3 race nicely at Lingfield on her previous run and looked fantastic in the paddock.

As the race unfolded I was clearly watching a different one from punters betting in-running because Christophe Lemaire, on Sabana Perdida, was always watching Heaven Sent and wanted to challenge late. For me, he was always going to reach Heaven Sent and then either get past her or not get past. I thought it was roughly evens whether Sabana Perdida did or not yet, in-running, Heaven Sent was 1.02 and Sabana Perdida 50-1. I wasn't confident that the French horse would win but she certainly wasn't 50-1. Yet I didn't back her in-running, although episodes like that make me wonder how I could possibly fail to win betting in-running.

I know I can because, when I've tried, I have, spectacularly. I'll get two races right then lose it all on the next one, and throw my toys out of my pram. I've no intention of trying again, even though it sometimes looks like easy money. I can't believe the prices people are prepared to offer and take.

Evidently the serious in-running punters are finding it harder nowadays. They used to be able to back a horse at 5-1 on when the horse was three strides from the winning line whereas, now, they are faced with 20-1 on with a furlong still to go. As in all markets, the windows of opportunity eventually close, as the market corrects itself. For my sake, it's probably just as well.

I think Duke Of Marmalade is a proper Group 1 horse, the

real deal, and I had £3,000 on it at evens. As they turned into the finishing straight, and Johnny Murtagh started to get serious, I was a bit worried but only briefly. It was soon clear that his mount was much better than his rivals, some of whom were running over the wrong trip while others just weren't good enough.

The first half of the card had gone near perfectly; the second half went less well. A lot of people would not back a 13-8 favourite in a 29-runner Royal Hunt Cup but if you believed, as I did, that Bankable was already a Group 3 horse running off a handicapper's mark of 94, plus a five-pound penalty, it was good value. His new handicap mark was 113. I thought the only thing that might beat Luca Cumani's horse was the fast ground. I had £3,000 to win.

Bankable was drawn 25 and I am at a loss to understand why Frankie Dettori and the other jockeys drawn high didn't race down the far side. In yesterday's Windsor Castle Stakes, with 25 runners, they raced in three groups and there didn't appear to be a significant draw bias. Yet Frankie and the others switched across the track and ended up in the middle, which wasn't going to make things better. To be fair, I think Dettori was the least to blame because he was on a horse who needed to be held up and he didn't have any choice but to go where the others drawn near him went. Bankable beat those drawn high and finished fifth, with the first four home all drawn low, but I am not convinced that they would have beaten Bankable if he had stayed on the far side.

The market was certainly right about Bankable being

a certainty on handicap ratings. When he next ran, in a Listed race at Newbury, he showed that he was well worth his new rating of 113, narrowly failing to give 8lb to a filly rated 115. That filly was Passage Of Time, who was subsequently narrowly beaten in the Group 1 Nassau Stakes at Goodwood.

Bankable's defeat wiped out my Duke Of Marmalade profit, and it didn't get better. In the Queen Mary Stakes, I backed Sugar Free, who finished fifth, and Danehill Destiny, the favourite, who, like Aqlaam, is trained by William Haggas. Danehill Destiny was soon last and stayed there. Finally, I backed Shabiba in the Sandringham Handicap, who finished third at 7-1.

For me, the good things all happened in the first part of the afternoon and, fortunately, were good enough to leave me still nicely in front on the day. It ended, as days at Royal Ascot tend to, with partying in Car Park 1. At one point I thought I might be rustling in the trees with trainer Vicky Haigh but she soon put me straight about that. I can't remember exactly how the evening ended, but not well.

*

THURSDAY JUNE 19

Dave Gorton's helicopter will be landing soon. It's another important day for us, with both Flashmans Papers and Elegant Cad running in the Norfolk Stakes. There are so few Group races for two-year-olds over five furlongs that it makes sense to run Flashmans Papers again. I wish they would move the

Norfolk Stakes to Saturday because you might then get more two-year-olds running twice at the meeting, just as Australian sprinters like Takeover Target have been doing in Tuesday's King's Stand Stakes and Saturday's Golden Jubilee Stakes. It would generate more interest.

All my colleagues in the press room have been telling me that the Windsor Castle wasn't much of a race and that Flashmans Papers will be out of his depth but he did pass virtually the whole field to win and Bushranger, who finished second, is highly thought of by his connections. A month after Royal Ascot, Bushranger won a Group 3 race in Ireland and then finished third in the Group 1 Phoenix Stakes at the Curragh, with Art Connoisseur, the winner of the Coventry Stakes, just in front of him.

Flashmans Papers was improving. On the evidence of their home work, Elegant Cad was probably the better horse, with more scope, but Flashmans Papers was streetwise, which counts for a lot.

Today, the stalls will be in the middle of the track. Flashmans Papers is drawn on the far side but he may be a horse who doesn't go fast in the first furlong, which will make it easier for Steve Drowne to decide where to go. Whatever the other runners do, they will probably do it in a group, so Drowne could have the decision made for him.

The favourite, South Central, is rumoured to be the best two-year-old Howard Johnson has ever trained, a beast of a horse – the usual story – but it's difficult to put a value on his 13-length win in a weak maiden race at Carlisle. It's not going to be a big betting race for me but, perhaps with my heart ruling my head, I've backed both Flashmans Papers and Elegant Cad, who started at 10-1 and 14-1 respectively.

As they were going down to the start, commentator Simon Holt said that, if Flashmans Papers won, it would be the first time in living memory that a two-year-old had won two races at the same Royal meeting, which gave me a tingle and made me imagine the headlines.

It didn't happen and, although they both ran well, Flashmans Papers finishing fourth to South Central, beaten one and a half lengths, and Elegant Cad fifth, I felt deflated. Gorton picked up a bit of prize-money and, with Flashmans Papers, was in the winner's enclosure again along with the first three horses, but the feeling was nothing like the one we'd experienced after the Windsor Castle Stakes. It brought home to us the enormity of Tuesday's win, so maybe it kept things real. We had a bottle of champagne but the atmosphere was subdued.

The Ribblesdale Stakes passed me by, then I backed Coastal Path, at too short a price, in the Gold Cup, and also had a small each-way bet on Geordieland. The ground was probably too fast for Coastal Path, who never looked likely to win but I thought Shane Kelly gave Geordieland a fine ride, and that his critics were very unfair. Circumstances conspired against Kelly. I'm sure he didn't want to take the lead as early as he did but the alternative was to take a pull which would have disappointed Geordieland, who probably wouldn't have picked up again. Once in front, Geordieland predictably felt he'd done enough and Yeats is such a galloper and battler that he wore Geordieland down. The right horse won. It was a great result for racing, with Yeats completing an Ascot Gold Cup hat-trick and yet another Group 1 success for Coolmore.

They have huge resources and the best equine blood but they still have to train and place the horses, and get the results, and they do. Punters might ask where the value is in backing Aidan O'Brien's horses but there is plenty of value in being in the payout queue after every Group 1 race, and they are winning most of them.

My biggest bet of the day was always going to be on Collection in the Hampton Court Stakes. Trainer William Haggas was clearly impressed when Collection won his previous race at York, and so was I. With the handicapper having raised him 13lb, Collection had to improve significantly to win, but I thought he could, and had £800 each-way at 13-2 plus a bit on Betfair.

Kerrin McEvoy rode Collection as if he always expected to win and, although Ascot's short finishing straight always makes me a bit nervous when a horse is held up, it worked out splendidly. Thank heavens.

*

FRIDAY JUNE 20

Three evenings carousing in Car Park 1 followed by getting up early for fear of missing a betting opportunity took their toll. On Friday I sat at home and watched it on television.

I thought Cuis Ghaire, who had already won a Group 3 race in Ireland, was a certainty in the Albany Stakes but she was also 11-8 on. Mark is more against backing short-priced horses than I am and I was expecting resistance to the suggestion that we back Cuis Ghaire. Fortunately, when I spoke to him, Mark said he thought the favourite should be 2-1 on. Thank God for that, I thought, we don't need to mess around trying to find a horse to back each-way, that is going to finish fourth. We had £1,800 on Cuis Ghaire and, from the comfort of my armchair, I never felt the need to raise myself from the horizontal to the vertical in order to help things along by screaming at the television. At 11-8 on, it wasn't a life-changing bet but it was nice to get a winner in the bag early on.

Earlier, after I'd done my telephone tipping line, I'd been for a walk. For the first few hundred yards, I fancied Bronze Cannon for the King Edward VII Stakes, for the next few hundred, I fancied Conduit, and then I started thinking that one of the three Irish-trained runners would be involved in the finish. It was that sort of race, which was just as well because the last horse I would have backed was the winner, Campanologist.

Frankie Dettori pleased the crowd by doing a flying dismount and it was the right thing to do but it is sad to see him doing a flying dismount after winning a Group 2 race for Godolphin, rather than celebrating a Group 1 victory. Maybe Godolphin will do better next year, when the effects of their latest buying spree feeds through, but I'm not sure how much that will change things.

Having agreed on Cuis Ghaire, Mark and I disagreed on the Coronation Stakes. Mark wanted to be with Lush Lashes, who started at 5-1, while I thought the one-mile trip was short of her best, and wanted to back Infallible, at 11-2. Mark turned out to be right and, having backed both of them, we ended up making the princely sum of £100.

My staking performance was even worse in the Queen's Vase, a race I probably shouldn't have been betting on because, as every year, most of the field were 'chancers' at the two-mile trip. I didn't expect Patkai, the 6-4 favourite, to win as he did and also backed the runner-up, Amerigo, at 14-1. Somehow I managed to put £700 on each of them, which meant that I ended up winning only £350 for an outlay of £1,400. I was somewhat annoyed with myself.

I didn't give myself a chance to get more annoyed by having a bet in the last race, the Buckingham Palace Stakes, which was impenetrable, as proven by the victory of Regal Parade at 25-1.

*

SATURDAY JUNE 21

I watched from home again, which was a shame as things turned out. From some points of view they turned out wonderfully well and, from others, desperately badly; a bit like life.

The afternoon kicked off, not at Ascot but at Newmarket,

where John Best was running Relative Order in a seven-furlong handicap. The previous day, John and I had a long discussion about why it was that, although his horses were very fit for their first runs, jockeys regularly got off them and reported that they needed the run. I thought it was because John was now training bigger horses and feeding them more and they needed a race to augment their training at home. When he said that Relative Order, who hadn't run for nine months, was a big, round barrelled horse; that he couldn't get the condition off him, and that the horse's last piece of work hadn't been very good, I refrained from hitting the 60-1 available on Betfair, let alone taking the SP of 33-1. Instead, I backed High Standing and Noble Citizen. Perhaps I should have reminded myself that, before Relative Order had won a nursery at Ascot the previous August, also at 33-1, the trainer told me that he couldn't possibly win.

Noble Citizen finished third, High Standing second and, you don't need me to tell you, Relative Order swept past them both to win. I was speechless. There was no point ringing John to abuse him because I wouldn't have been able to get the words out. And punters think, if only I had inside information.

Whenever Best has a winner, everyone assumes that I have backed it to win a fortune. Sure enough, the text messages started to arrive – 'well done', 'brilliant', 'how much did you have on?' If I'd known that I'd soon be watching another 33-1 winner trained by John Best, unbacked by Dave Nevison, I may have put my head through the television screen. Instead, in mild compensation, I had £2,000 on Macarthur, at 11-8, in the Hardwicke Stakes, with Mark adding some more.

Then it was the Golden Jubilee Stakes. Four days earlier, Kingsgate Native had finished tenth in another Group 1 sprint, the King's Stand Stakes. There were some excuses. It was his first run of the season and Jimmy Quinn hadn't been able to get Kingsgate Native covered up. Best was adamant that it wasn't his true running, and that 33-1 was a ridiculously long price for him in the Golden Jubilee. It makes sense now but I wouldn't have backed him with stolen money then, and backed Marchand D'Or and US Ranger, instead.

Kingsgate Native had a better draw this time, in stall three, and Seb Sanders rode a brilliant race. Kingsgate Native was keen but Sanders was determined to get cover and he got it behind the ideal horse, Takeover Target. It was an exemplary ride and it was great to see John Best leaping around afterwards. I wished I was there, or at least leaping around in my living room.

It was a great result for the stable, and a measure of its progress. In 2006, Rising Cross finished second in the Oaks and won the Group 2 Park Hill Stakes, in 2007 Kingsgate Native won the Group 1 Nunthorpe Stakes and now Best had won another Group 1 race. Aidan O'Brien dominated the meeting but it was some achievement for a small yard to win two races at Royal Ascot. Everyone likes an underdog and John is very good with the press. Hopefully, the publicity will help when it comes to buying horses at the sales later in the year.

When the Wokingham arrived, it was impossible to ignore the fact that the first five horses home in the Golden Jubilee, in a field of 17, had come from the lowest five stalls. I fancied Big Timer and King's Apostle but they were both drawn high, in stalls 28 and 23 respectively, so I scaled down my bets and backed Intrepid Jack and Lipocco. Having earlier taken the view that there wasn't a significant draw bias, I was suckered into believing that there was. There wasn't, because Big Timer won, at 20-1, and King's Apostle was third.

It was turning into a stressful afternoon, with my bet of the day, Mad Rush, next up in the Duke of Edinburgh Stakes. Jimmy Fortune gave Mad Rush a good ride, giving his mount every chance of winning, but Ryan Moore was inspired on Sugar Ray, who won by a neck. A longer straight would probably suit Mad Rush, who was gradually wearing the winner down. The Ebor, perhaps.

It wasn't the end to the Royal meeting that I had hoped for and I couldn't help thinking that, when I am so closely involved with a stable that had two 33-1 winners and a 100-1 winner during the week, I should have ended up showing an overall profit of more than £9,000.

What Royal Ascot did do was make me feel, more than ever, that I want to concentrate on buying and managing good horses.

CHAPTER TEN

10

GOING NORTH . . . AND SOUTH

After a meeting like Royal Ascot, it is difficult to work up the same enthusiasm for Lingfield and Carlisle, which is where Bertie Southstreet last won, 16 races ago, in 2005.

Benny Southstreet was a character in Damon Runyon's Guys and Dolls, which I saw at the National Theatre in 1982, with Bob Hoskins as Nathan Detroit. There is a point in the musical when the gamblers sell their souls to the devil and write IOUs to him on the back of bookmakers' tickets. I was sitting near the front and, when the gamblers threw their tickets into the audience, I caught one with 'Joey Perhaps' written on the back. He was another Runyon character, and I named horses after both of them.

Joey Perhaps eventually won a race for Kylie Manser, at Bath three years ago, after I had given up hope, and I'd given up hope of Bertie Southstreet ever winning again, either. As a two-year-old, he ran well in the Listed National Stakes at Sandown. On Channel 4, John Francome said that, if there was one horse you'd want to take home from the race, it was Bertie Southstreet. I wish Francome had taken him home because the only race he ever won for me was a five-horse maiden race, at 5-1 on.

What made things worse was that Bertie Southstreet flew up the gallops at home and John Best regularly told me that he thought he'd win. After thinking that he'd win for three years, I decided I'd suffered enough pain and punishment, and sold him to Graham Godmon. He lives near the stables and regularly watches the horses work and must have seen what Bertie Southstreet could do. Bertie Southstreet must have realised that I no longer owned him and, on June 24, promptly won at Newbury at 12-1. I was at Sevenoaks station at the time and listened to the commentary on the phone. Two days later, Best had yet another long-priced winner when Sapphire Prince won unexpectedly at Great Leighs, at 14-1. I didn't back that, either.

The day in between, at Salisbury, was quite a nice one, although Lovington's ice cream van ('A taste of the West Country') has been replaced by a Mr Whippy van, which is not nearly as good. Mr Lovington, if that's who he was, served you an ice cream cone as if it was a work of art. He was unbelievably appreciative of your £1.50. Maybe he spent too long talking to his customers, and lost the franchise.

The Bibury Cup is always a good race and it didn't take long in the parade ring to confirm that Warringah, trained by Sir Michael Stoute and ridden by Ryan Moore, was a certainty. When I got back to the press room to check its price on Betfair, it was 13-8 on. I didn't think that was value so, thankfully, sat the race out. After looking as an odds-on shot is supposed to for most of the way, Warringah succumbed to Resplendent Light's late challenge.

Eddie Fremantle said that the reason Warringah was beaten was that there was a fierce headwind, which the favourite bore the brunt of. That was encouraging, because the horse I'd come to oppose, Isphahan, was a front-runner. What I hadn't realised was that his promising apprentice rider,

David Probert, was a meteorologist. He'd obviously studied the wind patterns and, instead of making the running, tucked Isphahan in behind, which probably contributed to the fact that he won, and I didn't.

The next day, Hurricane Hugo moved on to Warwick, to greet Deposer, one of Kent Bloodstock's two-year-olds. Deposer had been working impressively at home and we expected him to win, with trainer Henry Candy's Amour Propre the only obvious danger. I had £2,000 each-way on Deposer at 4-1 and another £1,000 to win. Amour Propre went off the 2-1 favourite, with Deposer at 11-4.

Amour Propre pinged out of the stalls and, although Deposer travelled well and, at one stage, looked as if he might catch the leader, he couldn't. This time, unfortunately, there was a tailwind instead of a headwind. Although it was disappointing that Deposer didn't win, it was a good debut. Amour Propre broke the course record for two-year-olds that day and, when he reappeared at Bath a month later, he broke the course record there, as well, so he was pretty useful. I still think Deposer is one of Best's best juveniles.

At the moment, Mullionmileanhour seems to be the best and I have had £400 each-way on him at 40-1 with Coral for the Group 1 Nunthorpe Stakes at York (later transferred to Newmarket) on August 22. That is the race Kingsgate Native won as a two-year-old last year and the official weight allowance for juveniles could be overgenerous. The official scale allows two-year-olds 24lb from four-year-olds, compared with 17lb on Timeform's own weight-for-age scale. In its *Racehorses of 2007* annual, Timeform's essay on Kingsgate Native describes the official allowance as 'remarkably lenient'.

Mullionmileanhour is due to run in the Group 3 Molecomb Stakes at Goodwood on July 29 and, if he wins that, he'll be a lot shorter than 40-1.

On Friday June 27 I went to Chester's evening meeting for a speaking engagement. It was an additional fixture, and a disgrace, with four of the unappealing six races having fewer than eight runners, including a three-runner claiming race. The weather didn't help but, by Chester's standards, the crowd was disappointing. If you put on poor racing, the public are less interested in going.

I didn't have a bet but stayed for the racing on Saturday, when there were again some small fields, and four non-runners in the five-furlong handicap. On tracks where the draw makes a big difference, which includes Chester, you are always suspicious when poorly drawn horses are withdrawn. In that race, with 13 declared runners, the non-runners were drawn 13, 12, 11 and nine. Later, in a seven-furlong race, two of the dozen declared runners were taken out, drawn 12 and ten. In every case, there may have been legitimate reasons but it makes you wonder.

There was a big Scoop6 that day. It included the Northumberland Plate, at Newcastle, in which I thought I'd found one, Gee Dee Nen. I had £1,000 each-way on him at

22-1. During the race, I thought Tom Queally must have been replaced by Jamie Spencer. Two furlongs out, Gee Dee Nen was nearly last and, when he did try to make ground, there was a wall of horses in front of him. To stand and know what is going to happen before the jockey realises it is a horrible experience. Gee Dee Nen finished faster than anything to not get fourth. He got fifth, instead.

When Gee Dee Nen next ran, at Ascot on July 12, Shane Kelly overcompensated and went too early, but Gee Dee Nen did eventually win for me, on Ascot's Shergar Cup day, August 9. This time it was Hayley Turner on board. I had £1,000 at 7-1 and £400 each-way at 11-2.

Turner gave Gee Dee Nen a ride that was verging on being a candidate for the ride of the season, and one, in my opinion, that should have marked the end of Willie Carson's television career. As captain of the Great Britain team, Turner was under additional pressure. She brought Gee Dee Nen with a perfectly timed run, got stopped but managed to pull the horse out and really drive it to the line, to win by a head. With more luck, she would have won easily. On BBC, Carson couldn't resist saying that Turner rides pretty well for a girl, which is such an outdated and unacceptable attitude.

Gee Dee Nen gave me a decent win but a losing Scoop6 again took care of my winnings. It is becoming a habit.

After racing at Chester on June 28, I got a lift back with Damian Walker, the Tote's spokesman. There was one winning ticket in the Scoop6 and Walker was hoping that it would be held by a £2 punter, another Agnes Haddock. As we were driving along, he got a call from the Tote. 'Is it a £2 punter?' Damian asked.

'No,' said the man at the other end, 'it's a syndicate.'

'Do you know who it is?'

'No,' said the man, 'but I think it's your fucking mate, Dave Nevison.'

'It fucking isn't,' I shouted.

Mark and I had put £3,500 in the pool but the big syndicates, including Harry Findlay's, would have put in ten or 20 times that.

The next day, at Windsor, there was a Jackpot carryover of £54,370, which grew to £117,113. It seemed certain to be won because there were two odds-on favourites. The first race was won by Coole Dodger at 33-1, ridden by Gabriel Hannon(7). That knocked out virtually everyone and almost knocked us out, too. We had one ticket that included Coole Dodger, and we were lucky to have that because I almost included the whole field in that race, apart from Coole Dodger. Our remaining coverage was pretty thin; we just wanted the favourites to win, and the next two did.

When the final race arrived, we held 1.5 of the surviving 4.5 tickets. The situation was particularly promising because there was a strong odds-on favourite, French Riviera. The people holding tickets on French Riviera would normally hedge their position by laying the favourite, whose price would therefore tend to lengthen. We hedged at 4-6 but

French Riviera's price kept shortening, which suited us, because it meant that the favourite must be strongly fancied and we could lay it at an even shorter price. If French Riviera won, we'd win well over £20,000 and, if it lost, we'd win over £3,000. Unfortunately, it lost, badly, at 2-1 on. At the moment, I am massively up against it. I could really have done with French Riviera winning.

*

I was at Musselburgh's evening meeting on Monday June 30, working for Racing UK. Sadly, Freddie Williams was missing from the betting ring, having died recently. He was a fantastic bookmaker, and a maverick. I've no idea whether or not he made money as a bookmaker and I don't think we'll ever know. Freddie certainly wasn't infallible but he was unstoppable. If he got one wrong, he'd just plough on. The waves might be crashing over him but, like King Canute, he'd keep trying to push them back.

Williams didn't rely solely on his bookmaking business for a living and, when JP McManus wanted £100,000 on something, I think Freddie just rang up the water bottling plant he owned and told them to turn the taps on a bit more.

If a punter went up to him with a mobile phone clutched to his ear, Freddie wouldn't take his bets because the punter was using him to arbitrage on the exchanges, backing a horse with Williams and laying it on Betfair, and Freddie wouldn't tolerate that. Because he bet to his opinions, his prices would sometimes be much bigger than on Betfair, and he didn't want arbitrageurs undermining his business. I think he was right.

With Freddie and Pat Whelan gone, the characters in the ring are getting older and fewer. Tommy Morton is still there. I remember a group of City friends going to Scotland to have a touch on their horse, who was 25-1. One of them went up to Tommy and asked for £25,000 to £1,000. Tommy took the bet and left the price unchanged. The City man was puzzled, and checked to make sure that Morton had got him down for the right horse. 'Yes, sir,' Tommy assured him, 'that's it, £25,000 to £1,000. Would you like the same again?'

As the characters disappear, they will be replaced by young accountants, simply running a business. Like a lot of things, it's not the same.

I was going on to Hamilton the next day, again to work for Racing UK, and needed somewhere to stay overnight, so I asked Darren Owen, a racecourse commentator, and Ken Pitterson, a paddock judge, where they were staying. They were staying at a Travelodge on the M74. I asked them to book me in, too.

Since the last race at Musselburgh wasn't until 9.25pm, and the Travelodge was an hour's drive away, I wasn't expecting there to be any dancing on the tables, although I was hoping for at least some entertainment before bedtime. It was only £58 for the night but there wasn't even a phone in the room to ring the Samaritans, and no bar. There was nothing to do at all. I sat in the hotel and died of boredom.

Darren and Ken probably didn't mind, because other people's idea of an enjoyable lifestyle seems to be different from mine. Ken is a horseracing nut and travels with a case full of form books, and probably a few anoraks, as well. While I was wondering if it was worth getting a taxi into town, he was probably studying.

In the morning, I got up early and went to have breakfast at the Little Chef next door, although that caused problems because I hadn't got the voucher you needed to allow them to serve you sausage, egg and chips. I wasn't allowed to pay cash but had to go back to the reception desk at the hotel, pay for a voucher, and try again. I didn't have a *Racing Post* to read because, although I could see Hamilton racecourse in the distance, when I asked for one at a service station a few hundred yards away, they looked at me as if I was from another planet.

Darren and Ken were planning to set off for the racecourse at about 11.30am. I didn't think I could survive that long, and persuaded them to go earlier, which also gave me an outside chance of fulfilling my ambition to arrive at a racecourse in Scotland before Bill Harvey. Harvey works for BBC Scotland and is rumoured to sleep in racecourse First Aid rooms. You can never get to the press room before him and, sure enough, when we arrived he was already there. I think he must have a set of press room keys.

Bill is amusing but sometimes irritating, and thick-skinned, as befits a man reputed to have once stood as Conservative candidate for the Gorbals district of Glasgow. If he could knock on doors there when wearing a blue rosette on his blazer, he must be made of pretty strong stuff.

When I am appearing on television, I tend to put three or four bets up on Betfair and leave them. I'd had a small bet on Deep Winter, who won at 6-4 on, although only after being awarded the race following Jollyhockeysticks' demotion by the stewards. I was surprised that Jollyhockeysticks lost the race but, in terms of injustice, far worse things happen earlier on in races than during the finish. Quite often a horse suffers significant interference and loses its chance of winning but nothing is done about it. You cannot promote a horse who eventually finishes fifth but it is not equitable.

While the stewards were deliberating, we were talking to Richard Fahey's travelling head man. As well as Deep Winter, Fahey had runners in all four remaining races. The head man chatted away happily about the first three but, when we asked about Optical Illusion, in the last race, he was very vague. They hadn't had the horse long, he hadn't really seen it, they were just finding out. All of which was doubtless true. It was the same when we talked to Optical Illusion's jockey, Paul Hanagan. He couldn't tell us anything about the horse, either.

Optical Illusion had previously been trained by Ed Dunlop, then by Ian Semple and Linda Perratt. The four-year-old was now having his first run for Fahey and, having spent most of his career racing over distances from seven furlongs to nine furlongs, was racing over six furlongs for only the second time. Fahey is a fine trainer of sprinters.

Shortly afterwards, Racing UK interviewed Fahey himself. When he was asked about Optical Illusion, it was a similar story. He didn't know much about the horse. Someone thought they knew something, though, because Optical Illusion opened at 5-1 and was quickly backed into 7-2. I thought it was close to being a good thing, and backed it. I don't know how good it was but it was good enough to win, which was good enough for me. I didn't stay at the Travelodge that night.

CHAPTER ELEVEN

DROWNING IN THE POOL

My son bought tickets for the Iron Maiden concert at Twickenham on Saturday July 5. They were worth a lot more than the ones Mark and I bought for the Scoop6 the same day, even though our tickets cost more to start with.

It was Coral-Eclipse day at Sandown but before getting annoyed with myself for failing to back Mount Nelson in the big race, I got annoyed with myself for banking on Hoh Mike, a perennially slow starter, in the first race. He started slowly, and finished third, sinking our Scoop6. Please stop me backing Hoh Mike again, or going to Iron Maiden concerts.

The Jackpot wasn't won at Ayr the next day, which meant that over £92,000 was carried forward to Windsor's Monday evening meeting, when the pool reached more than £212,000, and again wasn't won. I congratulated myself on not having played, because I wouldn't have won it, either.

As it was pouring with rain at Windsor, I decided to find out what conditions were like for the meeting at Pontefract the following day. The way I did it was to ring Vicky Haigh, who trains not far away. It meant that I could find out about the weather (it was pouring down) and Vicky's wellbeing, a subject dear to many men's hearts. As well as telling me about the rain, Vicky told me that she would win the first race at Pontefract with Rosabee. She advised me to look at Rosabee's form.

I did as I was told, observing that Rosabee hadn't cost much, 4,400 euros, and didn't seem to have done much so far to inspire confidence. I told Vicky to enjoy whatever it was she was drinking but not to have too much more of it. Then I got back to the serious business of studying the Jackpot.

Mark and I put almost £3,000 into the pool, which grew to over £520,000. The first race, Rosabee's race, was a nursery. I thought Johnmanderville, the second favourite, was the most likely winner, followed by Predict, the favourite. Both ran stinkers and the race was won, by four and a half lengths, by Rosabee, at 33-1. We didn't have her in a single line.

It wasn't even a fluke. Rosabee won her next two races and then finished second in a Group 3 race at Ascot.

I felt a bit better after backing Hevelius at 12-1 in the next race, and a bit better still after Heritage Coast was beaten at odds-on, which would have sunk our Jackpot even if we'd included Rosabee. It sank everyone else's, too, because more than £520,000 was carried over to the first day of Newmarket's July meeting.

When there is that much in the pot it is difficult to resist but when the card is hard you have to be bold or it becomes horrendously expensive. The second race was a 20-runner six-furlong handicap for three-year-olds, where we wanted to have a lot of the horses covered. So, in the first race, a 13-runner handicap, we made Red Dune, the 11-8 favourite, a banker. All the signs were that she was better than an 83-rated handicapper, I thought she was the most solid bet of the day, and she represented the Michael Jarvis-Philip Robinson combination, one of my favourites when the circumstances are right. We put £2,500 into the Jackpot and, in effect, were having a £2,500 bet on Red Dune. When she won, I felt very pleased with myself, for a while.

In the second race, we had 14 of the 20 runners. We didn't have Spanish Bounty, the 33-1 winner, and that was that. The Jackpot wasn't won and almost £870,000 marched tantalisingly on to the second day of Newmarket's July meeting.

I wasn't there to see Red Dune and Spanish Bounty win, having gone to Lingfield hoping to see Deposer confirm his promising debut at Warwick a couple of weeks earlier. The market signs were favourable; Deposer was 7-4 on with no sign that anything else was particularly fancied. To my surprise, John Mayne, Kingsgate Native's owner, was there. When I asked him why he wasn't at Newmarket, John told me that he'd come to back Deposer. I should have doubled my bet, because Mayne is one of the luckiest men in the world. If he fell out of a 20th floor window he'd go up rather than down, and if he was backing the horse, it was a certainty. Sure enough, Deposer buzzed in. The plan now is to go for the Gimcrack.

These are interesting times for Kent Bloodstock and this season's experiences make me more and more attracted to the idea of focusing on the bloodstock side of things. The betting side is certainly hard work at the moment. On Thursday, the Jackpot pool reached almost £1.7 million. We played small and, from necessity rather than conviction, had Bouguereau, the evens favourite, as a banker in the first race.

He never looked like winning. The Jackpot was finally won, with 4.5 winning tickets, each worth almost £270,000. We seem to be good at putting money into the pool but not so good at taking it out.

It's frustrating and I'm coming round to the view that the chance of my winning £1 million in one hit is getting less and less. If Mark and I win when there's a huge pool, putting in a few thousand pounds, one of the big syndicates is very likely to have won, as well. We might end up being one of 20 winners, with Harry Findlay holding six of the winning tickets. We are better off, I think, concentrating on the days when there is about £60,000 in the pool, when the syndicates may ignore it.

Over the last three months, I have won over £30,000 on Betfair, which translates into a good year, but it has been swamped by losses on the Jackpot and Scoop6. Going for them is proving very expensive but equally worrying is the mental and emotional impact. It is demoralising and draining and, although I'm a resilient person, it gives you a huge negative feel. Doing the daily grind of fixed-odds betting gets harder and harder when, despite doing well at that, you end up writing out a cheque. A bad day at the office affects all of us and I am not immune from that. I react to good days and bad days and it has an effect on how I am with other people.

I feel a bit like the slot machine player who is reluctant to leave the machine because he fears that, as soon as he does, someone else will sit down and the three cherries will finally come up. It is difficult for me to walk away from a strategy that I think is sound and rational. The results on Betfair show that I am doing things right; my phone service is showing a profit; yet I am potless. Perhaps I should concentrate more on Betfair and on the front end of the market, partly because it is mentally uplifting to be in the payout queue regularly. To some extent, I am already doing that, although my biggest successes still tend to be with horses in the 4-1 to 12-1 price range.

Mark is even keener than I am to stick with our pool betting strategy. We don't think our approach to staking and perms is wrong; we have tried to be rational and prudent. What is wrong is that we haven't won a big pot and failing to do that has cost us a lot of money.

Although I am doing well on fixed-odds betting, the margins are getting tighter and I am on the brink of adjusting the way I use my tissue. My approach has always been that I have faith in my tissue and that, after allowing for a margin of error from ten per cent to 15 per cent, I will back horses who are bigger prices in the market than on my tissue. Provided my tissue is an accurate guide to each horse's chance of winning, the prices I take in the market represent good value and, over time, will produce a profit.

The only thing I don't know at the time I construct my tissue is how market sentiment will evolve. I am reaching the conclusion that the market has become such an accurate predictor of race outcomes that I need to be more responsive to what the market is saying. For instance, in my tissue for the Old Newton Cup at Haydock on July 5, I had Mad Rush at 100-30. I thought he was a handicap good thing and backed him at 4-1, which was a 20 per cent better price, and then for a bit more at 7-2, which you could say was breaking my own rules, except that my rules aren't set in concrete. When his price shortened still further, to 5-2, I stopped backing him. Instead, I backed a couple of horses who I'd priced up at 12-1 and were available at 20-1 or more. As a result, when Mad Rush won, my net profit was only £100.

Perhaps what I should have done was tell myself, Mad Rush is a 100-30 chance yet the market, having initially treated it as a 4-1 chance, is now insistent that it has a much better chance than that, and a much better than 100-30 chance. Perhaps this was a situation where I should have backed a horse even when it was trading at a shorter price than in my tissue, something at odds with my established approach, and something I am reluctant to do. Even so, I am tempted, and it was interesting to read Tom Segal, Pricewise in the *Racing Post*, arguing in the Weekender that no-one knows better than the collective wisdom of the market. That wasn't true a few years ago but I am beginning to think that it might be today.

The market is different from pre-Betfair days. It is now an amalgam of the best racing brains in the country and it reflects horses' true chances of winning more accurately than ever before. I have to come to terms with that and try to use it to my advantage rather than stick two fingers up at it. There isn't much profit to be made from following the crowd but if the crowd is the one that forms the market, which means Betfair, then instead of being against the crowd I have to try to be ahead of it.

I think that, more than before, in decent-quality races horses who drift from their morning prices don't win while those who are already prominent in the market and shorten further, do. Those price movements represent market sentiment, as opposed to the opinions of individual odds compilers, and market sentiment has become a more important factor.

I am doing some research to see whether or not the facts support my theory. If they do, then I may be better off accepting shorter prices than I have done in the past on horses who have shortened 'through' my tissue price and backing fewer horses at longer, drifting prices. In other words, if a horse goes through my tissue price in a positive direction, I will still want to be with it whereas, if a horse goes through my tissue price in a negative direction, I should leave it unbacked. That may mean missing out on some long-priced winners, which will take some of the fun out of it but, in this new world, in the robust markets associated with good races at major meetings, you don't bet against collective knowledge. Reading the market is very important as well as reading the form.

The fact is that, in terms of beating the market, my day

has slightly gone. Punters are better educated and better informed than they used to be, and there are fewer mugs. While my profile in the game has become higher, and brought me other sources of income, it has become harder for me to make money from punting.

I now look back affectionately at my early days as a professional punter, walking up and down the bookmakers' rows, betting in cash and settling up after each race. Eddie Fremantle and I were betting our opinions against the bookmakers' opinions, when some bookmakers still had them. When we backed a horse, they would often cut its odds, not because we had had a massive bet but because they respected our opinion, and they often accepted our bets on that basis. They wouldn't let us win too much but they tolerated us winning to help them make sure that other punters didn't. We did their work for them but now the only opinion that matters is the one they can all get by logging on to Betfair. My opinion is just one more opinion in the Betfair pot. It is slightly depressing.

So was Sayif's short-head defeat in the July Stakes at Newmarket on July 10, and Steele Tango's half-length defeat 35 minutes later, at 16-1, although I'd backed him at 25-1, and texted trainer Roger Teal to say that I thought his horse was a good bet at that price. You can be right, yet end up wrong.

The next day, I thought Kingsgate Native was good value in the July Cup at almost 9-1 on Betfair, and backed him to win £12,000. I also thought that Marchand D'Or was a real danger and might win but was not good value at 5-2. If you are backing a sprinter at that price, I would rather back one who is a straightforward ride, rather than a hold-up horse who might run into trouble. In the event, Marchand D'Or got there just in time while Kingsgate Native finished fifth, beaten only one and a half lengths. I think he has still got a good chance of winning the Nunthorpe again.

A week later, I was back at Newmarket's July course, where Girls Aloud were playing at one of the course's Friday evening concerts. Singing wasn't the name of the game but they looked gorgeous, like Lara Croft lap dancers made good. Max Mosley would have loved their costumes.

CHAPTER TWELVE

GLORIOUS GOODWOOD – YEAH, RIGHT!

You just can't help some people. I may be one of them. If I was still at school a teacher could make me write out, several hundred times, 'I must not bet at Redcar'. It might work.

It's too late to avoid the damage done by backing Mohanad in a seven-furlong maiden race there on Sunday July 20. After finishing second to Wildcat Wizard at York, Mohanad had finished third when odds-on at Salisbury. The horses who beat him had since run well, while Wildcat Wizard had won again. I thought that Mohanad should be 5-2 on rather than 6-5 on, and I had £4,000 on Mick Channon's two-year-old.

I listened to the commentary while driving my kids to a church hall, where they were performing in a play. Mohanad was the first horse to be mentioned. Unfortunately, he wasn't mentioned again. I couldn't believe it. He had to be involved in the finish, surely?

Had he broken down? Had the commentator mistaken his colours for those of the 20-1 winner, Quatermain? Would the commentator soon announce an amended result and offer his abject apologies?

It wasn't completely impossible. Many years ago, on holiday in Cornwall, I was in a betting shop in Falmouth when they announced a case of mistaken identity and corrected the result. I particularly remember, because I had backed the 'new' winner. Admittedly, that was a long time ago, before televisions were allowed in betting shops. I waited in vain for the announcement that the winner at Redcar was, in fact, Mohanad. No, Mohanad somehow managed to finish ninth of ten, murdering our small Jackpot perm in the process. I sat in the church hall and seethed.

*

Two days later, things looked up. Square Eddie was running in a six-furlong maiden race at Salisbury.

Dave Gorton was unable to be there but three mates of mine, more bar enthusiasts than racing enthusiasts, were planning to attend. They missed the train, which gave me a chance to study the card. When a man carrying a *Racing Post* told me how much he'd enjoyed reading *A Bloody Good Winner* I felt obliged to chat to him. He was an older man who had given up his job in the City and was trading on Betfair. His approach was very different from mine, but he seemed to be prospering. His method was to lay horses who couldn't possibly win.

He goes through every race and writes down the names of all the horses who, in his opinion, are no-hopers. Then he looks at Betfair, and lays them. He'll be delighted if he can lay one at 50-1 and, although the market is usually very thin, he has so many bets that it all adds up to a decent sum. That day, every horse he laid was beaten, and he ended up making about £500, without even a slight scare.

We expected Square Eddie to win but the usual rumours were circulating. Richard Hannon's Retro was said to be strongly fancied, and Terry Mills's Auld Arty was Listed class, although it didn't matter what class he was because he got in a state and wouldn't go into the stalls.

In the morning, I had £2,000 on Square Eddie at 9-4 and the same at SP, which was a mistake because, in the racecourse ring, he opened at 2-1 and was backed into 6-4. Judged by the way he won, even that was a generous price. He stretched out and quickened well. His sire is Smart Strike, the sire of Curlin, winner of the 2007 Breeders' Cup Classic and 2008 Dubai World Cup, and we are thinking of running Square Eddie in the Group 3 Sirenia Stakes on Kempton's Polytrack on September 6, although I think he will be even better over further, and perhaps on a more galloping track.

Square Eddie certainly didn't lack verbal encouragement at Salisbury. Afterwards, I collected the trophy on Gorton's behalf but it went on an awful lot of trains and taxis before it arrived home, at 4.30am.

*

GOODWOOD
TUESDAY JULY 29

With Flashmans Papers due to run in the Molecomb Stakes on the opening day of Glorious Goodwood, I was excited, but not nearly as excited as some of the jockeys in the opening race, a ten-furlong handicap.

There was nothing unusual about Seb Sanders riding Caravel for Sir Mark Prescott, since Sanders is the stable jockey, but it was significant that Sanders was riding Caravel even though he was unlikely to be able to do the weight,

8st 5lb. He managed to get down to 8st 7lb. I backed Caravel and Proponent, then watched them both in utter disbelief.

Levera and Luberon, habitual front-runners, went off like scalded cats and took each other on for the lead. That wasn't particularly surprising but what was amazing was that Sanders on Caravel and Steve Drowne on Proponent, both normally sensible, reliable jockeys, chased the suicidal pace. I quickly knew that I'd done my money but, in my usual fashion, instead of making a dash for Betfair and laying them both in-running, I just stood there in a stupor. Sure enough, both horses faded in the closing stages but my conviction that they were the right horses to back, or would have been if ridden more soberly, was reinforced by the fact that, while Levera and Luberon occupied the last two places, Caravel and Proponent still managed to finish sixth and seventh, in a field of 17, beaten less than seven lengths. I tried to console myself with the thought that they might represent good value next time they ran. It was poor consolation.

Then it was the Gordon Stakes, in which Conduit was 2-1 on. I thought Bouguereau was good value at 14-1. He had been outstayed over slightly further at Newmarket on soft ground and I thought Goodwood might suit him. Others agreed because he started at 10-1 but my optimism took a turn for the worse when I overheard the horse's connections talking to jockey Alan Munro in the parade ring. They told him that not enough use had been made of Bouguereau at Newmarket, and he was to make the running. Oh, no,

I thought. So he made the running, straight into a strong headwind, and finished fourth. Not for the only time in recent weeks, I wasn't in the best of moods.

That was partly because, when Flashmans Papers walked out of his box that morning, he was lame, having bruised his foot. He travelled to Goodwood with his foot in a poultice, then stood in the racecourse stables with his foot in a bucket of ice. On television, John Best told viewers what the situation was. It was a difficult decision to make but the horse was sound again and we decided to run him. In hindsight, it may have been a mistake. Flashmans Papers was drawn on the wide outside, which didn't help, and after getting close to a challenging position, he flattened out and finished sixth of 11, with Finjaan the winner. Under the circumstances it was a creditable effort but still disappointing. The plan is still to run him in the Nunthorpe.

*

WEDNESDAY JULY 30

Howdigo was another on the growing list of long-priced winners trained by John Best but not backed by Dave Nevison. This time it was at Windsor on July 14. Howdigo had been disappointing and, although I knew that he would probably improve for the big step up in trip that day, to a mile and a half, he hadn't been showing enough to justify putting my hand in my pocket, or my finger on a computer key. Howdigo won at 33-1.

Now he was running in a heritage handicap at Goodwood,

over the same trip. When I studied the race I found several form lines that gave Howdigo an excellent chance. I organised the troops and, although it took some doing, we eventually got about £1,500 each-way on, at an average price of about 20-1. It was a 16-runner handicap and bookmakers don't want to accept each-way bets on those races at one quarter the odds the first four places. As I have remarked before, those terms have virtually disappeared from the racecourse ring, where one fifth the odds is now standard. Barry Dennis and Colin Webster still offer the old terms but I think Webster does it as a loss leader, to attract customers who will then have other bets, and I won't ask Dennis because I'd just get a cartload of abuse. I've got some sympathy with his attitude because I rarely have win bets with him nowadays and it must be irritating if a customer only bets with you when the odds are in his favour, which they are in 16-runner handicaps, at one quarter the odds a place.

By the time I got to Goodwood, three of the 16 runners had been taken out, which meant not only a deduction from any winnings under Tattersalls' Rule 4 but that Howdigo had to finish in the first three rather than the first four for bookmakers to pay out on the place part of our bets. Howdigo started at 10-1.

Hayley Turner was riding and, in the parade ring, I told her that there looked to be plenty of pace in the race, that Howdigo would definitely stay the trip and that he had a real chance of winning. She was obviously surprised to hear that because, in the papers, Howdigo was an outsider. I told her to ignore that. Hayley seemed to take us seriously and she certainly followed our instructions perfectly. Once again, some experienced jockeys went off at a ridiculously fast pace and, after a couple of furlongs, the field was well strung out. At one point Howdigo was so far back that I wondered if he could possibly win from there but when I looked to see which horses were with him, they were horses ridden by Johnny Murtagh and Ryan Moore. Since, between them, Murtagh and Moore had so far won half the races run at the meeting, I decided that Hayley couldn't be doing too much wrong, and so it proved. Murtagh won the race on Love Galore with Howdigo finishing third. When she came back, Turner told us that Howdigo would stay further.

The problem with an each-way bet, even at 20-1, is that it only really pays for one more each-way bet. It won us a decent amount of money but not enough to have us doing high-fives in the winner's enclosure.

From a social activities viewpoint, the trouble with Goodwood is that, unlike Chester or York, everyone is spread out. Most people stay in little villages where nothing is happening, unless Miss Marple happens to be visiting. In earlier days, I used to stay in Bognor Regis, much favoured by ladies who work for the Tote at Goodwood. Some of them have been going for much longer than I have and after 35 years of smoking 40 Park Drive a day has taken its toll, they somehow don't look the same. This year, I'm going home every day.

*

THURSDAY JULY 31

We saw a contender for the best ride of the meeting in the first race, the Group 3 Moet Hennessy Fillies' Stakes over one mile and six furlongs, and it was on the runner-up, Folk Opera.

I felt sorry for Frankie Dettori because he gave Folk Opera, who hadn't raced over as far before, a brilliant front-running ride, slowing the pace down round the bends then kicking on a furlong out, only to get chinned by Gravitation, who he had never quite managed to shake off. It was another disappointment for Godolphin and, when Dettori came in, he looked as if he was wondering, what do we have to do to win? They got their just reward the next time Folk Opera ran; Frankie won the Group 2 Darley Prix Jean Romanet on her, at Deauville, over ten furlongs.

At Goodwood, one disappointment was immediately followed by another, for both Godolphin and me, when Dandy Man finished only third in the Audi Stakes. It was the seventh time that Dandy Man was a beaten favourite and he's a horse I clearly got wrong, to the tune of £2,000. I thought he was a Group 1 horse in a Group 3 race, but I was only right about the second bit. You can make excuses for him but I now think that Dandy Man doesn't want to do it and needs to be given the sack. If I back him again, I'll sack myself.

The day wasn't a great vindication of my judgement, since I joined other members of racing's intelligentsia in believing, for reasons that I find hard to remember, that Yeats could be beaten in the Goodwood Cup. Since John Mayne, the luckiest man in the world, was in the same camp, I thought I must definitely be right.

We stood in the champagne bar and, when the race started, John punched the air and shouted, "Right, let's get this thing beat." Six of us who had laid Yeats then watched him stride majestically to victory, by a contemptuous seven lengths. It wasn't financially disastrous because Yeats was 15-8 on but it did make me wonder what I was doing standing with a glass of champagne in my hand. What was I celebrating? You have to admire a great horse, I suppose.

Any competent jockey would have won on Yeats but Johnny Murtagh, who did, is absolutely in the zone at the moment, constantly in the right place at the right time. Riding for Aidan O'Brien is a huge advantage but Murtagh has ridden winners for other trainers at Goodwood, too, including a fine ride on Baddam in yesterday's Goodwood Stakes. He rides at this meeting every year but he doesn't ride regularly at other Goodwood meetings and still outshines jockeys who do.

Sometimes you can be too close to a yard or a horse and that may have lured me into having £600 each-way on Bertie Southstreet at an average price of about 28-1 in the closing sprint handicap. He started at 14-1.

My theory was that, with Bertie Southstreet's win at Newbury the previous month, we had finally worked him out. He was a sprinter with a relatively high cruising speed but no turn of foot. What he needed was to follow a fast pace. When those in front of him weakened, he wouldn't quicken but he would keep on at the same pace, which would be fast enough to put him in front. Drawn high, Jimmy Quinn tracked Merlin's Dancer and eventually went past him on the far side but the first five home raced on the near side. Bertie Southstreet finished ninth, beaten not much more than three lengths.

I felt that the theory was sound but the execution less so, and tried to suggest a race that would suit his requirements. Sandown was a candidate because they tend to go a fast pace there and race in a single group. Bertie Southstreet visited Sandown on August 13, and finished fourth of nine. Maybe the steady pace was to blame, or perhaps the soft ground. There is another explanation; maybe he's simply a rogue.

*

FRIDAY AUGUST 1

I wasn't at Goodwood but at a studio in Wapping, where I was appearing on a new sports betting television channel, SportsXchange.

Having decided to do the Jackpot at Goodwood, where there was a carryover of £95,136, I was on the telephone, putting the bet on, when a light started flashing with the message that we were on air in two minutes. It was a bit fraught.

During the finish of the second race, I cheered as Pearly Wey just got up to beat Baby Strange by a nose, at 10-1, because the winner was in my Jackpot. I realised something was wrong when the Tote put up details of the number of tickets going on to the various runners in the next race. For some of the horses, I was holding more live tickets than the totals on the screen. I checked my selections, which I had written down, and Pearly Wey was one of them. In the rush, there hadn't been time to read through the bet again. The woman who took it must have taken down the wrong number. I put in a phone call, but I knew there was nothing that could be done. It cost me more than £30,000.

That was Friday, and it was a pretty miserable one. That was before Saturday arrived.

*

SATURDAY AUGUST 2

I was in Sevenoaks, looking after my wife's cat and trying to win the Scoop6, which had over £600,000 in the win fund. We bet £1,500. Four of the races were from Goodwood, and two from Newmarket. The first one, from Goodwood, was one of the most difficult and we included six of the 13 runners in our perm, including John Best's Southpaw Lad, who was 25-1. Southpaw Lad had never raced beyond a mile and was now running over 11 furlongs. On breeding, he was far from certain to stay the trip and I didn't think he would, but Best insisted that Southpaw Lad looked and ran like a stayer. Best was right, Southpaw Lad did stay and knocked out all but a few hundred Scoop6 tickets.

It was too early to get excited but we comfortably survived the next two legs, won by a 5-2 second favourite and 5-1 third favourite. Then it was the Group 1 Nassau Stakes at Goodwood.

Independently of the Scoop6, I had £888 on Lush Lashes, the favourite, at 5-4. Kevin Manning gave the Coronation Stakes winner a poor ride but several other jockeys didn't shine, either. Yet again, Johnny Murtagh demonstrated his superior skill, setting a dawdle that suited his mount, Halfway To Heaven, then sitting on the leader's shoulder while the others got in each other's way off the pace. He is at the top of his game and of his profession at the moment.

Halfway To Heaven won by a head but, although she showed herself to be game and willing, I don't think she was the best horse in the race. She won thanks to Murtagh. For me, there was some consolation because Mark and I had the winner in our Scoop6. When I looked to see how many tickets had survived, it was 30, of which we had 21. Just two legs left. Now I was getting excited.

The fifth leg was a six-runner handicap at Newmarket. We had the front three in the betting. Should we hedge? The odds were shorter than 5-2 on that one of the three would win. If it had been the final leg, we definitely would have hedged, but the final leg was the 27-runner Stewards' Cup. If we hedged, and one of our three won, it could become messy. We didn't hedge, and the Newmarket race was won by Bee Stinger, at 9-1, which we didn't have. The only consolation was that Conquest then won the Stewards' Cup at 40-1, although we would certainly have been able to make a profit of some sort by laying some of our seven selections.

I lay on the settee, went to sleep and didn't wake up for two hours. I was emotionally drained. We had been so close to finally landing a big Scoop6.

The following day, I went with Natalie, my girlfriend, to see a film called Man on Wire, about Philippe Petit's amazing tightrope walk in 1974 between the World Trade Centre's twin towers. I sat there, still in an emotional state, mesmerised. Natalie said, 'Do you think he's ever fallen off?' I looked at her and replied, 'Yes, he did once, but he was lucky, I caught him.' It just seemed so ridiculous, both him half a mile up on a wire, and me and the Scoop6.

CHAPTER THIRTEEN

FLYING TO FLORIDA

There are few better feelings in horseracing than the feeling that you have information that very few other people have got. It is such a good feeling that most punters would rather hear what a horse's trainer or jockey thinks than study the form, even though the connections' thoughts are usually not worth knowing and the punters would be better off learning what the form has to say instead.

If all inside information was in the public domain, there would hardly be any price fluctuations and horseracing would be like virtual racing, Portman Park brought to life. Unless the market is woefully weak, a horse's price doesn't tumble from, say, 8-1 to 5-2 just because someone takes a particular view of the horse's chance of winning, based on its form, unless the someone is the Sultan of Brunei, and he has become an avid form student. The price tumbles because some people believe that the horse has a better chance of winning than its odds suggest, with their belief based on inside information, sound or unsound.

At Kempton on August 6, John Best was running Black N Brew in a nursery in which one of the other runners was Red Humour, trained by Barry Hills. Hills owned the horse in partnership with Ronald Arculli, a former chairman of the Hong Kong Jockey Club. Red Humour had won its previous race and stood out in the parade ring, although looking very green.

As Jimmy Quinn, who was riding Black N Brew, walked into the parade ring, he looked at a Chinese gentleman who was standing with Charlie Hills, Barry's son, then walked up to him and shook his hand. Evidently the man was John Chan, formerly Arculli's deputy and now himself chairman of the Hong Kong Jockey Club, a very influential position. It looked as if Chan was en route to the airport and Hills seemed to be telling him, jokingly, that the trophy for winning the race would fit into his small bag. Perhaps they were all particularly keen to send Chan on his way celebrating a success.

Was this inside information, or information in the public domain? Did it explain why Red Humour's odds tumbled to 5-2 favourite? I know I would have been better off without the information because I backed Red Humour on the back of it. He ran green and finished fourth, two places behind Black N Brew.

I don't think that strict regulation of inside information of a positive kind will give the public greater confidence in the sport's integrity, and result in them betting more, but I do respect what the authorities are trying to do in relation to negative inside information, particularly in highlighting the laying of horses whot have been stopped.

*

After Elegant Cad had finished fifth in the Group 2 Norfolk Stakes at Royal Ascot, we took him to Maisons-Laffitte for the Group 3 Prix du Bois. He ran disappointingly on the softish ground and we decided the immediate priority was to win a race with him. The race we chose was a maiden at Wolverhampton on Monday August 11. It was a far cry from Royal Ascot and, unsurprisingly, Elegant Cad was 11-4 on.

I always feel a bit uncomfortable when I'm involved with an odds-on shot because you are on a hiding to nothing. Maybe I was seeing things that weren't there but I thought there was a possibility that Elegant Cad might turn out to be one of those horses who runs well whatever standard the race is but ultimately disappoints; one of those frustrating horses who finishes fifth in a good race and then, when dropped in class, finishes fifth in that, too. Dave Gorton, the owner, was on the phone while I was in the parade ring and I was thinking, if this horse loses, I'm going to have to explain why.

Mercifully, that wasn't necessary, although Elegant Cad made hard work of winning, just holding off Layer Cake. My immediate reaction was disappointment that he hadn't won more easily but the runner-up was a nice looking horse and may prove to be quite good; I see that he has been entered for the Group 2 Mill Reef Stakes on September 20. Seb Sanders, who rode Elegant Cad, was also encouraging. The way the race unfolded meant that he was forced to make the running. He told us that Elegant Cad would be much better suited to running down better horses than trying to boss lesser ones, as he had to today. What Sanders said made sense.

I know that, if he had been beaten, it would have been a long journey home, with a tricky conversation with Gorton for company.

*

OCALA
MONDAY AUGUST 18

It is always nice to leave Wolverhampton and, a few days after leaving it, John Best and I flew to Orlando, Florida, about 4,200 miles from Wolverhampton's Dunstall Park. When we got there, John informed me that he hadn't brought his driving licence with him, so I had to drive from Orlando to Ocala. I am not the most confident driver on the US side of the road and my passenger didn't look quite so perky when we arrived at the Hilton in Ocala where, every time we got into the lift, a voice announced, 'horses stay for free'.

We were there for the bloodstock sales where, last year, Elegant Cad was one of our purchases. Ocala calls itself the horse capital of the world. I'm not sure how many people outside Ocala also call it that but we think it's a good place to go for reasonably priced yearlings.

I did manage to get Best drunk that evening, which I've never managed to do before, but there was a high price to pay. He spent the whole of the next day complaining that he'd got a bad stomach and, whenever we started talking to any women, he'd introduce himself by saying, winningly, 'My name's John. I'm really tired.'

His stomach certainly wasn't as bad as the one hauled down to breakfast each day by a man mountain wearing a pair of shorts that could have accommodated an armchair in each leg. Mount Rushmore started his day off by putting half a dozen sausages and half a dozen rashers of bacon on a plate, along with a pancake, then melting three balls of butter over the sausages. It was like watching Homer Simpson in an eating competition.

As a young man I used to think that Americans were over the top and insincere but, although for most of them the world doesn't seem to stretch beyond the USA, I have now started to like them, and think they tend to be naturally warm and friendly.

We went to O'Malley's Alley and Tin Cups Tavern to see exactly how friendly they were. The Alley and the Tavern cater for people my age, 46, and rather older. It was great fun, with live bands playing music from the sixties, seventies and eighties, and everyone getting up to dance, but it involved negotiating some severe shocks. Golden deceivers were everywhere and Ocala turned out to be the spiritual home of the breast implant. I don't think there was a woman there over the age of 30 who hadn't had a boob job, and there were a lot of women a great deal older than that.

You'd stand behind a woman with beautiful long blonde hair and, when she turned round, with you awaiting the arrival of a goddess, you found yourself staring, instead, at something usually found hanging up in a hut in Papua New Guinea. It was unnerving, as was the sight of women with arched backs and hunched shoulders sporting enormous breasts and massive cleavages. It was unreal, as were they.

We tried the Midnight Rodeo, which catered for younger partygoers. As the neon sign reading M - d n i - - t Rodeo suggested, it wasn't the classiest of establishments. There were a lot of very drunk people although, judging from the size of the security men, there probably wasn't too much trouble.

There was a country and western section where all the men were wearing check shirts, cowboy hats and spurs. They clearly weren't there to socialise with anyone not wearing the same uniform. As we walked out, the line dancing started. It was like watching a Louis Theroux programme – seriously weird. About 100 cowboys were line dancing to U2 music. It was great to watch but made me feel as if I was visiting an alien society. There was no way you could walk up to someone and talk to them about it.

Given the economic climate, I thought there might not be too many buyers to compete with at the sales, and there weren't. When we went to the sales complex, it was disturbingly quiet, not just because of the state of the economy but also because Hurricane Fay was on its way. Judging by the reports in the local media, Armageddon was on the doorstep, with advertisements on the radio for insurance, and counselling. On the other hand, someone told me that, if I'd ever stood on the top of a hill in Yorkshire, it would be pretty much like that.

Having already studied pictures of the horses online, we diligently studied them in the flesh, and went to bed early on Sunday night, ready for the select sale the next day, August 18.

Ocala has a large, indoor, air-conditioned auditorium, which is needed given the heat and humidity outside. We were quite worried that the sale might be cancelled because of the threat of a hurricane and, judging from the anxious looks on some of the vendors' faces, they were worried that it might not be. One of them told me it was going to be 'a pinhooker's paradise'. There certainly weren't a lot of buyers and exactly 50 per cent of Monday's 230 lots were either withdrawn or not sold. Those that were sold fetched an average of $50,243, compared with $57,961 the previous year, a drop of 13 per cent.

We bought four yearlings, each costing between $25,000 and $30,000, but got into trouble on one we were trying to buy for Harry Findlay, a colt by Limehouse. We were told that the reserve was $70,000. The bidding duly reached $70,000 and Best bid $72,000. The auctioneer had been taking bids from us regularly but claimed not to have spotted that one, and brought the hammer down at $70,000. We were screaming and waving but it didn't do us any good.

As we followed the horse out, in the hope of doing a deal if the vendor had bought it back, Harry was also screaming, down the phone. He was probably waving as well, on his boat in the Mediterranean. The horse finally arrived at a spot where a small woman, aged about 60, as wide as a stable door, was standing, covered in an expanse of denim. Nearby was her husband, Jack Sprat, whose dinner she must have stolen every night for the last 20 years. His mouth was like the ones worn by men in spaghetti westerns. When he said something, which wasn't often, his lips kept moving afterwards, but very slowly.

It was difficult to find out exactly what they wanted. It seemed to be $100,000, although I'm not sure they'd have accepted it if we'd offered it. Harry was screaming, 'Offer them fucking 80.' The Beverly Hillbillies were expressionless, absolute granite, definitely not for turning. All I know is that, according to the sales results, the horse had been sold to Seasoft Stable for $70,000.

At the sales, I find that you can get into a mindset where you find yourself agonising and haggling over relatively small sums, even though you know that the selling price represents good value from a buyer's point of view. When we go to the Doncaster Sales later in the month, I expect similar horses will fetch the same figures in sterling as they were fetching in dollars at Ocala. Even after the travel and other costs, I think there was value there.

We did a good day's work on Monday but not enough of it. I am a risk taker by nature and would have bought a few more but Best is more cautious, conscious that, when we've bought them, we've got to find someone to buy them from us. Even so, the next morning I think he probably also felt we could have been bolder and, having not intended to go to Tuesday's less select session, we did. We bought two more yearlings, one for $10,000 and the other for $20,000, with a view to capitalising on the weight allowance they will receive in maiden auction races. It was exciting; auctions are.

*

Back home, I have been doing a bit more work on my theory that I need to take more account of market sentiment than I have done in the past. The market is now such an accurate predictor of the outcome of races that, as I have suggested before, if a horse goes 'through' my tissue price in a positive direction, it may be in my interests to carry on backing it whereas, if a horse goes through my tissue price in a negative direction, I should leave it unbacked. Over the years, that is not what I have done.

I have been looking at the morning prices for races with more than £10,000 win prize-money. Those prices represent the opinions of odds compilers and changes to the prices during the run-up to the race reflect market sentiment. If market sentiment has become as important a factor as I believe it has, horses who shorten in price will do well while those who drift will do poorly. It is early days but so far, particularly in the case of 'drifters', the results seem to support my theory. Where there is a perceived opinion that a horse should be, say, 5-1, as indicated by the odds compilers' prices, and it is 7-1 at the off, indicating negative market sentiment, the horse won't win.

For instance, at Newmarket on August 22, in the rerouted Yorkshire Oaks, Passage Of Time was 7-2 in the morning but then drifted out to 6-1. Mark and I laid it, and Henry Cecil's filly finished a well-beaten fifth of six.

The previous evening, admittedly in a low-value apprentices' race at Chester, the early prices for Zennerman and Feeling Fresh were 3-1 and 9-2 respectively. In my tissue, they were

5-2 and 7-2. I backed both of them, having £300 on each. Market sentiment towards Zennerman remained positive – he started at 5-2 – but was very hostile to Feeling Fresh, who drifted to 8-1. Was it significant? Well, Zennerman won and Feeling Fresh was last of the 14 finishers. In the old days, as Feeling Fresh's odds drifted further away from my tissue price of 9-2, I would have continued to back it; not now.

I don't think drifts of that kind necessarily indicate that something is amiss but they do suggest that someone who is influential in the market strongly believes that the horse's chance of winning is a lot less than odds compilers and myself believed it to be a few hours ago. It may be because of the state of the ground, or because the horse has not been working well at home. There is some negative information expressing itself in the market and, more than ever before, I need to pay heed to it.

An hour after Passage Of Time ran disappointingly in the Yorkshire Oaks, Kingsgate Native and Flashmans Papers ran in the Nunthorpe Stakes, also rerouted to Newmarket. Since John Best was going there, I represented the yard at Newbury, where Deposer ran in the diverted Gimcrack Stakes. After being a bit keen early on, he did well to finish sixth of 12 to Shaweel but perhaps Deposer was a bit overfaced and it might have been better to have found an easier race for him. Sometimes it is difficult to decide whether to go for the big one, which is terrific in every way if it comes off, or concentrate on getting wins in the bag.

One thing the Gimcrack proved was that I have a misguided idea of how old the occupants of the press room are. When Marine Boy, the 11-8 favourite, was well beaten, I remarked to the journalists occupying the same lift as me, 'Well, Marine Boy obviously forgot to take his oxy-gum.' I expected everyone to fall over laughing, in as far as they could fall over in the lift. Instead, they all responded with bemused stares. I thought everyone knew that Marine Boy was a cartoon character who, thanks to oxy-gum, could breathe underwater. As a child, I used to dream of being Marine Boy. They obviously didn't.

I have rarely seen a horse run as fast as the South African challenger National Colour ran in the Nunthorpe, just getting caught by Borderlescott, who broke the track record. Kingsgate Native is fast but he was off the bridle by halfway and most of the rest of the field were completely outpaced including, regrettably, Flashmans Papers. Kingsgate Native did well to finish third while Dandy Man reinforced my growing conviction that he doesn't try hard enough.

CHAPTER FOURTEEN

THE NEW WORLD – KEENELAND

B uoyed by the feeling that we may have bought some bargains at Ocala, John Best and I set off for Doncaster's St Leger Yearling Sale. For the first time in England, we decided not to employ Highflyer Bloodstock as our agents, although some of John's owners, in the Heading for the Rocks partnership, continued to do so. I don't suppose Anthony Bromley and David Minton, of Highflyer Bloodstock, were very pleased with our decision because they have a good record for us but we feel we now have the experience, working as a team, to do the work ourselves, and reduce the costs. If the yearlings we buy turn out to be useless, we may have proved ourselves mistaken, but I think it will work well. In future, we expect to use agents to sell horses for us rather than buy them.

We went up to Doncaster on Sunday August 24 and, over the next few days, looked at every single horse, all 500 of them. After Ocala, it was nice to go through the catalogue and have heard of most of the horses in the pedigrees, which meant that we were armed with more knowledge than in Florida. It may not have made too much difference because our approach is to concentrate first on each individual horse's physical merits, or otherwise, rather than on its pedigree.

It was disconcerting to see so many big Newmarket trainers there already but the pain was eased by the eve-of-sale champagne party. Admittedly, we had to listen to Henry Beeby, the sale company's managing director, talking about the new sales complex but then we could drink as much as we liked. Champagne reaches your brain pretty quickly and, halfway through the evening, I decided it was an appropriate time to let Vicky Haigh know what she'd been missing out on. After harassing her for an hour and refusing to take no for an answer, she finally dumped me unceremoniously, not in the best of humours, at the St Leger pub. It was a bit of a disaster on several fronts. First of all, I didn't feel very well afterwards and, second, whenever I ring Vicky, her phone now identifies me as 'Deluded Dave'.

Things went better in the sales ring, where we bought five yearlings on the first day, including a colt by Choisir for 60,000 guineas. That yearling, and three others, were bought for John Mayne, who will not have Kingsgate Native racing for him next year, having sold his champion sprinter to Cheveley Park Stud.

In the evening, Con Marnane, a leading Irish pinhooker, invited us out for a Chinese meal. Con is a lovely man and has been a big help to John and me. We piled into a cab with various other Irishmen and headed into Doncaster. As readers of *A Bloody Good Winner* will know, Doncaster is not my favourite destination and, on this particular Tuesday evening, it excelled itself. Apart from the lack of sunshine and absence of a beach, it was Tuesday night in Alicante, with hordes of girls dressed in their best, displaying vast expanses of artificially tanned flesh. When I expressed surprise that the town was packed on a Tuesday, the taxi driver said, 'Oh, no, luv, it's always like this on a Tuesday night.'

After the meal, I was supposed to be meeting someone at the St Leger Tavern, which was difficult, because the locals disclaimed all knowledge of any such tavern. It turned out that everyone knows it as Biscuit Billy's. When I finally got there, at least there were no serious fights, except with Vicky. Success again had to wait for the sales ring. By the time the sale ended, on Thursday August 28, we had bought 15 yearlings, most of them with owners already lined up, and there was still the Keeneland Sale to come.

On Saturday September 6, John and I boarded a plane for Cincinnati, then drove to Keeneland, on the outskirts of Lexington. While we were in mid-air, Square Eddie, Flashmans Papers and Deposer all ran in the Group 3 Sirenia Stakes at Kempton. It is the only Group race in Britain for two-year-olds on Polytrack and, with American tracks switching from dirt to Polytrack or other artificial surfaces, we were advised by Kern Lillingston, an American bloodstock agency we have used, that the winner would be a very sellable commodity. His reasoning made sense and I thought Square Eddie was good enough to be the winner. I think he could turn out to be as good as Kingsgate Native.

I was planning to have £3,000 on him, until I saw the draw. Square Eddie was drawn two of 12. Icesolator, the only horse drawn worse, was withdrawn. The draw was a serious disadvantage, making it inevitable that Steve Drowne would have to travel further than his better drawn rivals. The previous day, the nursery run over the same six furlongs was won by Rocket Rob, drawn 12 of 12, with two horses subsequently withdrawn, including the horse drawn one. An hour later, the horse drawn one finished last in another race over six furlongs. It didn't inspire confidence.

I couldn't decide whether to go for glory, on the basis that Square Eddie would be good enough to overcome the draw, or back him each way. The other horses weren't mugs. Elnawin had just beaten 18 other two-year-olds to win a first prize of more than £160,000 in a sales race at Newmarket, while Weatherstaff had looked promising when winning on his debut at Ayr. I decided to have £1,500 each-way on Square Eddie, at 9-1.

Martin Smith, John Best's assistant, was representing the yard at Kempton, and Dave Gorton, Square Eddie's owner, was there. It was frustrating knowing that, while we sat in the plane, a race that was important to us was being run, and we couldn't watch it. Was Gorton clutching the trophy? As soon as the plane landed, I turned on my mobile phone. The first text message informed me that the phone company was going to charge me a fortune if I rang home; the second message read, 'great run'. As soon as I saw it, I knew we hadn't won. That's what 'great run' means; ran well without winning. Square Eddie, or one of Best's other runners, had run well, but hadn't won.

Square Eddie had been beaten a head by Elnawin, the favourite, after a neck-and-neck tussle to the line. It was gutting but Drowne told us that we had the best horse in the race, a serious horse, and that he would have won with a better draw. And I would have won over £16,000 instead of £1,200.

*

KEENELAND
SEPTEMBER 8 – 11

Harry Findlay wants us to buy a horse for him at Keeneland. He's arranged for credit of $300,000.

I saw Harry at Salisbury two days before we set off. He came up and asked what I thought of Cityscape's chance in the novice stakes' race for two-year-olds. There were only five runners but I told him that there were a couple of dangers, and Cityscape was only 11-10. 'It's absolutely on its own,' said Harry. 'I know it's fancied.' Cityscape won by nine lengths. 'Dangers?' said Harry. 'Fucking dangers? I tried to tell you.'

Harry's got a lot of bottle and will have a go and seems to be convinced of his own invincibility. He probably won £150,000 at Salisbury, while I was there working for Racing UK for £250. I don't begrudge him in any way, and it will be nice to have horses of his in John Best's stable.

Monday and Tuesday, the first two days of the Keeneland Sale, feature the most select lots, although in the USA, they call them hips. There's Sheikh Mohammed, and there's John Magnier, and there's Bradley Wayne Hughes, the 61st richest person in the USA, worth over $4 billion. If it comes to a head-to-head battle, we'll do our best, but it may be difficult. We know we aren't going to be able to buy the yearlings with the best pedigrees and, for the first two days, there aren't many without good pedigrees. We take comfort in the fact that people seem obsessed with pedigrees. People are buying horses for $400,000 that John Best and I wouldn't bid $40,000 for, because of their conformation.

We wander down to Barn 7 to see hip 237, a colt by Forestry out of Miss Zafonic, being sold by Kingswood Farm. It may be within our price range. The colt is walked out for us to inspect, a chestnut with a white blaze. John approves of the colt's freedom of movement through its shoulders. He says it is pretty correct; nothing major wrong. I put the colt down as being a relaxed walker, immature and leggy. It's a big learning curve for me, with John as my guide.

A little way along the same barn, another vendor, Gracefield, has slices of pizza laid out on a table, for potential buyers. Elsewhere, Taylor Made Sales Agency is famed for its cookies, Mill Ridge for its rum cake. I am a potential buyer and try them all. Very good, and free. We look at hip 284, another colt by Forestry, being sold by Gainesway. John notes that it is a decent size, with scope, its near foreleg rather offset, but a nice horse.

We walk back to the sales ring with a view to bidding for hip 116, a colt by Vindication, with a weak enough pedigree to give us a chance, perhaps. John is a very disciplined bidder, more cautious than me. Our target price is $100,000. The bidding starts slowly. A bid spotter, standing in an aisle nearby, beckons with his fingers – come unto me, all ye who are heavy laden with dollars. Best bids $80,000, then the bidding slips away from us, and the colt is sold for $170,000. We aren't going to chase the price because we want to buy horses for sums that give us a realistic chance of being able to sell them for more in the future. We have some wealthy owners to buy for but they are largely owners with a trading mentality. If we pay $300,000 for a horse, we want to feel confident that there is a good chance of turning it into a horse worth more than that. Our philosophy is to try to buy horses for less than they are worth, not for what they are worth. We want to feel we have got a bargain. There are so many horses here that, if we are patient, we should be able to find them. In the meantime, although it is interesting and fun, it is also frustrating watching horse after horse go through the ring without our being able to buy it. Next year, depending on what clients we have, we may decide to arrive later and stay later, missing the cream of the crop but here for the more affordable milk.

Hip 136 is next on our list, a colt by Eddington. Ryan Mahan, one of the auctioneers, is gabbling away tremendously fast from his seat on the podium, flanked by two other gabblers. It's impossible to understand what Mahan is saying, if anything. We have $100,000 in mind. Others have bigger figures in mind. BBA Ireland prevails, at $310,000, with the horse evidently going to trainer Karl Burke. Later, hip 237 goes for $100,000. We don't buy that either and, in the meantime, Hucking Harkness wins at Folkestone, at 14-1. Another long-priced John Best-trained winner I didn't back.

During the sale, there are a lot of people in Lexington, people who have money to spend and need feeding and entertaining, so I was expecting a bit of action on Monday night but we struggled to find it. We went to Harvey's Bar, where we were the only people there, had a quick drink, bored ourselves, and moved on to McCarthy's Bar, in South Upper Street. That was empty, too, possibly because, alongside the more traditional cocktails, like the Cosmopolitan and Manhattan, was something called the Car Bomb. It was made from Guinness, Irish whisky and Bailey's Irish Cream, which sounded explosive enough. It cleared us out, anyway, to the only slightly less frightening Mia's, just along the road, where there was supposed to be a midget lesbian karaoke competition. If there was, they must have been too small for us to spot them, or we'd gone the wrong night. We thought of giving Bang a go, but that turned out to be a gay club, so it all ended disappointingly quietly.

On Tuesday, we were already looking towards Wednesday. The most exciting news of the day was that we were getting offers for Square Eddie, including one of $600,000 for three-quarters of the horse, with a view to racing him in California, and aiming him at the Breeders' Cup Juvenile at Santa Anita on October 25. While discussing it on the phone with Dave Gorton, Square Eddie's owner, I told him that I hadn't checked to see what the limit was on his credit at Keeneland but assumed there wasn't one. Then I held the phone a long way from my ear. I'm not sure exactly what he said, but I'm pretty sure it wasn't, 'Yes, that's right.'

John and I went to look at hip 271, a colt by Smart Strike, Square Eddie's sire, but he went for $500,000. Instead of chasing horses beyond our reach, we concentrated on drawing up a shortlist for Wednesday and Thursday's auction. Then we headed for Malone's Restaurant and Oscar's oyster and piano bar.

Malone's claims to serve the best steaks in Lexington but so does every other steakhouse in Kentucky. I've taken to asking for the smallest steak on the menu, which isn't very small. If I don't see another steak until my next visit, I won't mind.

Con Marnane arrived brandishing the $100 he'd won at a raffle held by the Taylor Made Sales Agency although, judging by the regularity with which he wins it, I think there must be a lot of raffle tickets with his name on them. Richard Fahey arrived in Oscar's piano bar brandishing a set of drumsticks. It was a side of Fahey I hadn't seen before, although I don't think the regular drummer was too impressed. It was very amusing, if not very musical.

We've had to revise Wednesday's shortlist because of veterinary warnings about some of the horses, which we don't feel we can ignore. Harry Findlay's been on the phone, wanting us to look at hip 763, a colt by Proud Citizen, so we go to barn 32 and have it brought out for us. John isn't overly impressed. It has slightly long and 'sloppy' pasterns and walks very close in front. It's not good enough for us, but it's good enough to attract a bid of $525,000 from Blandford Bloodstock.

We are interested in hips 704, 727 and 797. We are also interested in hip 883, a nice chestnut colt by Elusive Quality out of an A.P. Indy mare. He is not the best of walkers but we still like him. Unfortunately, he seems to have attracted the interest of Sheikh Mohammed. I don't think he has to check his credit quite as often as we do, but we'll push him as far as we can. In the meantime, near barn 37, we've discovered some excellent cheesecake, great hot dogs and some fine salt beef sandwiches. I've rarely been so well looked after, or fatter.

John goes to $220,000 for hip 704, a colt by Dixieland Band, but the yearling is led out, reserve not attained, at $230,000. Hip 727 is a bay colt by Smart Strike, a sire we like. Scott Caldwell, a member of a family of auctioneers, is doing the gabbling, in a 1950s military crew-cut. The man sitting next to him has had his hair cut to look like Liberace, which may have been a mistake. The bidding quickly reaches $130,000. John attracts a bid spotter's attention, and makes the winning bid of $180,000. At last, we've bought one, and for $20,000 less than our target price.

There's a slight hitch. Someone tells us that we've bought a rig, a horse with an undescended testicle. We go to barn 34 to look at our purchase. John examines it, and arranges to have the horse checked independently. The vet declares that it is not a rig. Then it's back to the sales ring for hip 797, a bay colt by Grand Slam. Our target price is $130,000 and, this time, John makes the winning bid at $115,000. This is more like it especially as, the next day, a colt we like less, by the same sire, fetches $300,000. We stay on to wait for hip 883 but, as we suspected, John Ferguson is bidding for Sheikh Mohammed, and gets the colt for $375,000 – too much for us. Still, we are pleased with our buys and, on Thursday, we add two more, a Johannesburg colt for $130,000 and a Successful Appeal colt for $75,000.

At Ocala, Doncaster and Keeneland, we have bought a total of 25 yearlings. Next year is going to be interesting. Now, we have to find owners for all of them.

CHAPTER FIFTEEN

LOOKING BACK... AND FORWARD

The six months is up; the Lincoln to the St Leger. I set myself a profit target of £80,000 and, instead, I am about £80,000 down. It's not what a professional gambler expects, it's not what I am used to, and it's not much fun. £80,000 down, and that doesn't include the cost of living an expensive lifestyle for six months. I've had other, compensating sources of income, from writing, broadcasting, my bloodstock work and my telephone tipping service, which has been doing a lot better than I have, but my core income since 1993 has been gambling, and that has let me down. It has left me at a low ebb as far as my enthusiasm for betting goes. Losing does affect the way you feel.

I say that my gambling has let me down but it would be more accurate to say that part of it has let me down, the Tote part. I have made a profit of about £60,000 on fixed-odds betting, much of it on Betfair, but I've lost about £140,000 on pool bets. My profit from fixed-odds betting isn't as big as I'd like, reflecting the fact that the market has become a more difficult one, but it tells me that I haven't lost the plot completely. Betting from my tissue still enables me to win with great regularity, and winning regularly is therapeutic. Tote Jackpot and Scoop6 betting is different. Inevitably, most of those bets lose, which is demoralising, and quite often they lose in frustrating circumstances, which is doubly demoralising. During the six months, we haven't won a single Scoop6, although we've gathered a few hard-luck stories along the way. We have won several Jackpots but none of them has been a big one.

In effect, what I've been doing is winning £3,000 on Betfair or with bookmakers, then promptly losing £7,000 chasing a Scoop6 or Jackpot. Arguably, the rational thing to do would be to abandon the big pool bets and concentrate on fixed-odds betting, but I am reluctant to do that, partly because I want to win a life-changing sum, which is extremely hard to do betting at fixed odds, and partly because I still believe that the big pool bets represent the best value, as well as the best chance of a win that will make a real difference. I still think my approach is rational. Serious punters have a significant advantage over casual ones when doing the Scoop6 or Jackpot, so it makes sense for me to do them. Our £140,000 loss on Tote bets has to be put in perspective. It represents just one Scoop6 win or a couple of decent Jackpot wins. I don't think the losing run we have had on pool bets since the Lincoln is statistically significant. Of course, there is a danger that I will go bust before proving that I am right.

As far as fixed-odds betting is concerned, I still go to the races expecting to win and, more often than not, I do, especially at the big meetings. I still have an advantage over most other punters but it is not as big as the theoretical advantage I have in the big pool bets, nor is it as big an advantage as it used to be. Going racing and betting for a living is still a lovely life but it has always been hard work and, now, it is even harder. Maybe my appetite for work and my ability to stay on top of the huge amount of form has declined but, more importantly, I think I have enjoyed the benefits of a golden age of punting, a golden age that is coming to an end.

Betfair has been a great boon for punters but it has brought the best players together, which means that horses end up being the prices they should be, which reduces my winning opportunities. The mismatches I used to exploit between my tissue and bookmakers' prices are still there, but they are there less often, and to a less marked extent, than they used to be.

Betfair has also exposed the generosity of some established each-way terms, with the result that they are no longer available from most bookmakers for significant sums. On the racecourse, one quarter the odds the first four in handicaps with 16 or more runners has generally been replaced by one fifth the odds. Off-course, it is very difficult to strike a decent each-way bet, certainly on midweek meetings not on terrestrial television. You can get on if it is a 30 runner handicap but not if there are 16 or 17 runners. I remain convinced that it is only a matter of time before off-course bookmakers change their each-way terms, for the worse.

The whole market has been tightened up so that punters are turning over a lot of money but at worse margins. Now, Betfair has started to change its treatment of big, profitable players. As most of my exchange betting is backing rather than laying, I may not be directly affected but the days of being a professional gambler on the exchanges may be numbered, and it is certainly becoming more difficult. Over a five year period, Mark Smith and I have made approaching

£500,000 profit on Betfair but we have paid about a third of that in commission, even with a commission rate of between 2.5 per cent and 3 per cent. Mark has called an emergency summit meeting about the latest development, and it is certainly something we will have to examine. It may mean that we will use bookmakers more in future, although that means having money in a lot of different accounts, which is unattractive.

Betfair will have to be careful about how it treats the relatively small number of core clients who are responsible for a substantial proportion of its daily turnover on horseracing. I think it is on shaky ground if it thinks the punters likely to be affected by changes in their terms will just sit and take it. Those punters are very margin and profit sensitive and if Betfair upsets them and makes life more difficult for them they will explore other opportunities and other exchanges will try to lure them away. Betfair's position in the market is very strong but it isn't irreversible and if the liquidity of markets weakens, other options might begin to look appealing.

My approach to fixed-odds betting still works but, increasingly, I think I need to adjust it, and in a way that is difficult for me. Although I've got only a limited amount of research to back this up, I believe that market movements are now more significant than they used to be and that I have made less money than I could have done recently because I have continued to put my tissue before the market. As I have suggested earlier, I should probably give more weight to late changes in market sentiment and keep backing horses when they pass through my tissue price in a positive direction, while resisting the temptation to back those moving through my tissue price in a negative direction. I don't find that easy, because it involves reshaping my concept of value, and I am in a transition phase with it.

The secret of success in betting, as in financial trading, is having superior knowledge. One way of having that, as Harry Findlay has shown, is to buy horses and be prepared to run them against opposition you know is inferior then back them at short odds, knowing that their odds should be even shorter. It is something else I need to take on board, although having big bets on odds-on shots involves another difficult change of mindset for me. I've never liked that kind of betting but I recognise that a 6-4 on shot can represent good value.

This year, we've had some good two year-olds and I should have exploited my knowledge of their ability more than I have done, but backing unraced juveniles is fraught with danger, even if they have been flying up the gallops. Deposer was an example. He had been working very well at home and we fancied him to win on his debut at Warwick in June but, starting at 11-4, he finished second to Amour Propre, the 2-1 favourite, who won his next race and is probably useful. It was a good first run by Deposer, but it was a losing bet.

When I should have had a real go was on Deposer's next run, on Lingfield's Polytrack. We knew he was good – he was subsequently rated 94 – and he was running in a weak maiden race. He opened at 11-8 on and was backed in to 7-4 on. It certainly wasn't all my money causing the contraction but I knew, as far as you can know, that Deposer was actually a 5-1 on chance. If I was Harry Findlay I'd have had £50,000 or maybe £150,000 on Deposer but I haven't got that kind of money and I'm not in that zone at the moment. I think about what it would feel like if it lost. Of course, Deposer didn't lose, he won easily and, as time goes by, when I have that sort of advantage, because of my superior knowledge of the horses I'm involved with, I should exploit it. We'll see.

The opportunities should certainly arise because I am becoming more involved with John Best's operation and it is an expanding one. John and I have just returned from Keeneland with another four yearlings to go with the six we bought at Ocala and the 15 from Doncaster. We now have two versions of the Kent Bloodstock partnership, the owners of Deposer and Mullionmileanhour, with each version owning eight horses. If we can recruit more clients, there will be more partnerships.

I am managing Dave Gorton's horses, and hoping to find more for him. Gorton accepted an offer of $1 million for Square Eddie, from Paul Reddam, an American-based buyer, prior to him running in the $500,000 Breeders' Futurity at Keeneland on October 4. In that situation, it is always a difficult decision; to take a certain, substantial profit or shoot for the jackpot?

The day before the race, I was met by Joe Miller, who works for Kern Lillingston, the bloodstock agency that helped us when we bought Square Eddie. We were going to a cocktail party at Keeneland for connections of the runners. As I had only arrived in the US that afternoon, it was effectively midnight for me before we started, and I was a bit tired. That disappeared at the sight of a row of tables with Kentucky's finest food and drink for free. There were various martini glasses full of multi-coloured cocktails. I've no idea what they were but they tasted fantastic.

By 9.30pm, which is the time that most Americans seem to want to go to bed, any jet lag had gone and myself and two of John Best's staff, there to look after Square Eddie and other horses running at the meeting, went into Lexington. We ended up at Harvey's. As far as I am aware, we had a terrific night and I woke up at 10.30am the next morning, not long after I had gone to bed, with 36 missed calls from Best, all asking pretty much the same thing, 'what the fuck are you doing?' I got a cab to the track.

Elegant Cad got the ball rolling, badly, when knocking himself coming out of the stalls in the seven furlong allowance race. Later, we discovered that he was lame but, at the time, we wondered if the whole experiment was doomed.

We had three of the 11 runners in the Breeders' Futurity but, in our minds, Square Eddie had the best chance. Miller had booked the jockeys for us, with Rafael Bejarano, a rising star, on Square Eddie. In the paddock, all three horses looked well but Square Eddie looked outstanding. I had $300 on him on the pari-mutuel, at about 9-1, and £300 in England, at roughly the same price.

Watching the race, Square Eddie was never going to be beaten. He broke well, was positioned well, then kicked clear down the straight to win by almost five lengths. It was very impressive. Deposer ran well to be fourth, with Flashmans Papers, for whom the one mile and half a furlong trip was probably too far, finishing eighth.

We ran to the middle of the track to get the winner's blanket over Square Eddie, while the American media made a beeline for Doug O'Neill, who would be training the horse from now on. O'Neill seemed a very nice man and made a point of saying that he had only seen Square Eddie for the first time half-an-hour ago.

Reddam was thrilled, unsurprisingly, and so was Bejarano, who told me that Square Eddie had tremendous pace and quality and a lot of power at the end, and that he was really hoping to ride him in the Breeders' Cup Juvenile. I was thrilled, too, but although we had been advised that $1 million was an excellent price on the basis of what Square Eddie had achieved, and been offered less by high profile buyers, it was impossible not to wish, with hindsight, that Gorton had kept the horse.

I was inundated with congratulatory texts, including one from Harry Findlay, to say that he'd got nothing but admiration for us, and had had £2,500 on Square Eddie, on Betfair.

A few days earlier, Harry had decided to come on board properly as an owner with John Best, and we bought four horses for him at Goffs Sale in Ireland, including a yearling colt by Cape Cross out of a Sadler's Wells mare for 140,000 euros. Harry was massively enthused about that.

Among the yearlings we had vetted was a filly by Peintre Celebre out of a King Of Kings mare, submitted by the Irish National Stud. John and I both liked her, and the vet's report was positive. We expected to have to pay a fairly serious price for her but, when she walked into the ring, the auctioneer had to stoop down to 5,000 euros to attract a bid. John put his finger up for 6,000 euros and, to our amazement, that is where the bidding stopped. I know the economy's in a poor state, but we still have no idea why she was so cheap, except that it was quite a long walk to her barn; maybe not many buyers made it.

I rang Harry and told him, sorry, but you can't have that one, you can have half. I dipped my toe back into ownership and had the other half. It will be very interesting to see how she turns out. I expect she'll be useless, but maybe she'll turn out like Rising Cross, and cover herself with glory in the Oaks.

Altogether, we have now bought eight horses for Harry, and Best is his biggest trainer on the Flat. Some of them may end up being targeted at races in the U.S. We will certainly be studying their programme books carefully for next year, because there is a lot of prize-money and some fairly uncompetitive races.

After winning so well at Keeneland, Square Eddie ran even better at Santa Anita on October 25, finishing runner-up to Midshipman in the Breeders' Cup Juvenile, again showing a lot of talent and a good, battling attitude. A year earlier, Dave Gorton had bought his first horses, five yearlings. One, Flashmans Papers, had won at Royal Ascot and another, Square Eddie, been second in the Breeders' Cup, albeit in a new owner's colours. By any standards, it was an exceptional start. Hopefully, we will have found another Flashmans Papers or Square Eddie for Gorton next year.

I have tried to encourage a culture at John Best's yard of developing horses to sell, although it does become difficult when an owner has to decide between a good profit and the chance of glory. The idea is for John and I to work together as a team, buying yearlings and racing them, usually as two-year-olds, with a view to selling them on for a profit for their owners. I see my bloodstock work becoming increasingly important, partly because I think it offers a better chance of landing a jackpot for me than betting. With betting, to some extent, I feel I've been there, done that, got the proverbial T-shirt and, with margins deteriorating, I am ready to shift my focus. In future, I will be spending less time at racecourses and more time at Best's stable and at the sales.

My failure to land a big Scoop6 or Jackpot has encouraged that but I will carry on shooting at the big pools, although not at the Tote's new Super7, which has proved to be monstrously ill-conceived and shows the Tote to be so grasping and shortsighted that I can't see how the bet can survive. Someone at the Tote must spend hours scouring the cards trying to find the day's seven most difficult races, spread across two or three meetings, so that no-one can possibly win. Punters aren't as stupid as the Tote obviously thinks they are. If they think they've no chance of winning, they won't have a go at the bet but will simply consign it to the too difficult tray, which is what they have been doing since the bet was launched, at the start of the St Leger meeting. The Tote say they are promoting the bet but they are doing the opposite, by behaving as if they don't want anyone to win. They think it does them a favour if no-one wins, and the losing stakes are carried forward to swell the pool but it is the worst ever exercise in marketing.

The Super7 can't be promoted at a particular racecourse, because it is made up of races at several courses, and serious punters are put off by having to turn over a lot of pages of the *Racing Post* to find all the form. It is too much hard work for too little chance of success. The Super7 should build on the established success of the Jackpot and be a seven race bet at a single meeting, starting at race one and ending at race seven. All the Tote has to do is select the meeting. Wherever it was, an announcer could announce, 'We have the Super7 here today. It's your chance to win £100,000.' The Jackpot would have a 50p minimum stake while the Super7, a big bet with big dividends, would have a £2 minimum stake. Simple.

Unless the Tote changes the Super7, my go at it on September 26 will have been my last. That day, I won the Jackpot at Ascot, worth £6,723, and needed Isphahan, the 9-4 favourite, to win the last race at Haydock and win me the Super7. David Probert gave Shaman a great ride but was beaten a short-head by Just Bond. Harry Findlay was sharing the bet with me so, before Isphahan's race, I rang him, woke him up, told him the situation, and asked him to lay Isphahan for a few grand, which he did. It would still have been a lot better if Isphahan had won, which he did, at Ascot two days later.

I will still be going to the big meetings, which I love and generally do well at, but I will concentrate even more on the big races and good horses rather than the bad ones. This winter, I will be going jumping. The summer jumps horses will have disappeared, to be replaced by a body of horses that I will be able to get a handle on. That should help.

More interesting times ahead.

INDEX

Bee Stinger 192-193
Beeby, Henry 211
Bell, Andy 'Two Earrings' 102, 104,
    116, 123
Bell, Graham 102, 104
Bertie Southstreet 155-156, 189-190
Best, John 60-70, 76, 77, 78, 87,
        130, 134, 137, 139, 149-150,
        151, 155, 156, 185, 191, 197,
        206, 211, 215, 217, 231
    and Florida trip 71, 200, 201,
        202, 203, 204
    and Keeneland Sale 213,
        216-217, 218, 219, 220, 230
Betfair 40, 63, 66, 68, 77-78, 81, 113,
        172, 173, 175, 176, 227-228
    Cheltenham Festival 10, 15, 16,
        19-20, 24
    forum 10, 19-20, 105
Bethell, James 126
betting exchanges, arrival of 64
betting percentages 33-36, 37-38,
    39-40, 41
Big Buck's 53
Big Fella Thanks 65
Big Timer 151
Binocular 49, 50
Black N Brew 197, 198
Blandford Bloodstock 219
Blazing Bailey 49
Bloody Good Winner, A 33, 50, 87,
    182, 212
Blythe Knight 128
Bognor Regis 187
Bolger, Jim 132
Borderlescott 207
Bouguereau 171-172, 184-185
Boychuk 53
Bradburne, Mark 21
Brands Hatch half-marathon 61
Brave Prospector 45-46

Broadway 17-18 see also Dormy
House Hotel
Bromley, Anthony 69, 211
Bronze Cannon 147
Brunei, Sultan of 197
Buick, William 131
Burke, Karl 217
Bury St Edmunds police station 123
Bushranger 144

C

Cabinet 84-85
Caldwell, Scott 220
Campanologist 147
Camps Bay 95, 96
Canadian Danehill 85
Candy, Henry 157
Cape Vale 112
Captain Cee Bee 50
Caravel 183-184
Carberry, Paul 17, 28
Carnegie, Dale 9
Carson, Willie 159
Cecil, Henry 205-206
Celestial Halo 15, 26-27, 50
Cesare 137, 138
Chan, John 198
Channel 4 Racing 18, 155
Channon, Mick 181
Chapple-Hyam, Peter 45
Chartist 106
Cheltenham 28
    Montpelier Wine Bar 10, 19, 25
    Queen's Hotel 19
Cheltenham Festival 9, 10-29, 48-49
    Arkle Chase 11, 13-14, 17, 55
    Ballymore Properties Hurdle
        25-26
    Champion Bumper 24
    Champion Chase 21-22, 54